THE

INTRICATED

SOUL

ALSO BY SHEROD SANTOS

Poetry

Accidental Weather

The Southern Reaches

The City of Women

The Pilot Star Elegies

The Perishing

Essays

A Poetry of Two Minds

Translations

Greek Lyric Poetry: A New Translation

THE

INTRICATED

SOUL

NEW AND SELECTED POEMS

SHEROD SANTOS

W. W. NORTON & COMPANY

New York · London

For information about permission to reproduce selections from this book,
write to Permissions, W. W. Norton & Company, Inc.,
500 Fifth Avenue, New York, NY 10110

For information about special discounts for bulk purchases, please contact
W. W. Norton Special Sales at specialsales@wwnorton.com or 800-233-4830

Manufacturing by Courier Westford
Book design by JAM Design
Production manager: Anna Oler
Library of Congress Cataloging-in-Publication Data

Santos, Sherod, 1948–
The intricated soul : new and selected poems / Sherod Santos. — 1st ed.
p. cm.
ISBN 978-0-393-07216-7 (hardcover)
I. Title.
PS3569.A57I67 2010
811'.54—dc22

                                                            2009040991

W. W. Norton & Company, Inc.
500 Fifth Avenue, New York, N.Y. 10110
www.wwnorton.com

W. W. Norton & Company Ltd.
Castle House, 75/76 Wells Street, London W1T 3QT

1 2 3 4 5 6 7 8 9 0

FOR

LYNNE

CONTENTS

ACKNOWLEDGMENTS

Grateful acknowledgment is made to the editors of the following journals, in which some of the new poems first appeared: *Field*, *The Gettysburg Review*, *The Kenyon Review*, *Ploughshares*, *Raritan*, *Shenandoah*, *Slate*, *The Yale Review*.

The epigraph is from John Donne's *LXXX Sermons*.

Poor intricated soul! Riddling, perplexed, labyrinthical soul!

—JOHN DONNE

from

Accidental Weather

(1982)

THE ART OF CRUEL COLORS

At the touch of a match, the afternoon's heap
of colorless leaves goes up swiftly in a draft of smoke.
Does the eye offend less cruelly now

the season's flowers are blown? Twenty years ago,
Jacek Gruszka, an émigré welder
who lived next door, stepped from his side yard

garden shed, shaded his eyes against the sun,
then walked over to the heirloom roses
he'd brought from his family home in Prague.

Lifting up above his head a metal rake,
he battered the heavy looping canes, hauled them up
from the roots, then battered the roots as well.

After raking the leavings into a pile,
he returned to the shed, replaced the rake
on a shelving hook, and hung himself from a beam.

As if awaiting the arrival of whatever it was
his life outlived, the floribunda petals lay
scattered across his manicured lawn.

SIRENS IN BAD WEATHER

The wet streets are undisturbed by that chronic
   high whine, as of a fish hawk over the blue glaze,
over the moldering light that slips in
   through the clouds. A week's rain has pasted
litter to the sidewalks and grates, to the tires
   of the Groat's refrigerator truck which unloads
nightly in the alley below. And a melancholy
   damp now settles in the bones of the passersby
who await the hour of their enlightening.
   Their patience is the kind the Stoics believed
was proof of our eternal souls, though others
   still wonder what we're actually waiting for.
Take that man kneeling like a muezzin
   at the curb beside his crumpled car: his keening,
high-pitched wailing keeps imploring—no,
   demanding God reveal His terrible secret now.

ON THE LAST DAY OF THE WORLD

As usual, the guard who worked
the night shift at the boardwalk

returned home tired to his bed.
The sky began to whiten, a window

opened, and pigeons were squabbling
in the waterfounts. There were

fishermen smoking on the docks,
and someone was already swimming

when the sun appeared to sweep
the beaches clean of their debris.

On the promenade, shopkeepers
opened up early that day

(the tourist season in full swing),
and a pair of joggers

were cooling down in the water-
colored shade of the palms.

Then the bathers arrived
with their coolers and towels

to stake out spots in the sand,
to close their eyes on the sun.

And quietly, as though daybreak
had requested it, a radio love song

floated through the air. Too tired
to sleep, the guard turned over

on his side, seagulls made blue rings
in the air, and what else was there

to mark that hour but the fact
that it would never come again?

CLEARCUTTING

With the hammer and tongs of a diesel drill,
the rain forest wakens to new excavations,
the tumuli of forsaken gods turned out
for tourists from the cruise ships docked
in Cozumel. Each year, prosperity markets
its primitive appeal and iced-over drinks
and parasails perpetuate the thrill
of otherness tended like a putting green.
Last night we stood beside a waterfall
while torchbearers hauled up heavenward
on ropes slip-knotted around their feet
were spun above us in a breakneck, old-world
sideshow to that Mesoamerican history
the Julian calendar slashed and burned.

SELF-PORTRAIT IN A PARIS SUBURB

I'd taken the train to Enghien-les-Bains
where I telephoned for a taxi to the casino.
I'd stepped off the train in the evening,

the sun had set, and the shuttered windows
of the houses there seemed closed against
whatever the coming dark would bring.

Though the station platform was empty,
a loosening cloud of tule fog
moved back and forth across its boards

like a crowd of people patiently waiting
for another crowd of people to arrive.
Off to one side of the ticket gate,

a soiled, crib-size mattress (it all
seemed vaguely Russian at the time)
lay flat on the bed of a porter's cart,

though what memory clings to still
is the fact that its ruined fabric
was stitched with quilted air balloons.

An hour or so later, the waiter flung
a tablecloth out (was he humming
an American jukebox song?) and a woman

walked over from somewhere to say,
"You won't believe what happened to me."
And, as it happened, I never did.

BESIDE THE BLUE RIVER

on the drowning of a childhood friend

The summer house backed by a wooden
pier blistered from sun and gurry.

Tar pots posted at the washouts,
lories in the mangrove swamps.

Days I'd soon grow out of while,
planta non grata, as the guidebook said,

water hyacinth drifted down
from the flooding north

seeded itself along the waterways
and choked off what in other days

distilled to such translucent pools
we'd sight-fish wading into them

with handmade bamboo poles.
I hardly know the boy I knew,

but as I did, I cast across
his reflection, his wide eyes fixed

unblinking behind the scrim
of a world where sunfish glide

in and out of his shadow.

K.

My dearest Milena,
                    The stars tonight are beyond
my normally sober count. The city sweepers
neglect my street, and the air is rank with rotting stuff
vendors heap at the curb. Though you accuse me
of sounding lighthearted (and not the shadows cast therein?),
the truth of it is I rarely sleep, erratic pulse, little blood.
And when I rise in the morning, I'm as hollow
and insensible as the casing for a sausage from which
the meat's been scraped away. And so it is I ask myself,
how on earth did anyone ever imagine that people
can commune by post? Surely, written kisses
never reach the lips they seek, for along the way
they're drunk up by the nebulae of all those ghosts
we're haunted by. On this ample diet, mine, of course,
have multiplied so enormously that, like cats
to milk, they come sipping about my pen tonight.

The news? A review of my work has finally appeared.
What do you think of this: "Kafka's bachelor art"?
Apparently, my "art" must ape whatever it is
I think I'm not, so perhaps you'll take less seriously
that graphologic dabbler you keep "bumping into."
As you well know, I'm hardly a "budding sensualist,"
nor am I "determined in my behavior," even
"artistic interests" falls short of the mark, as anyone
could see from the artless way I address you
in these letters. But how is it you're unable

to gauge the effect that your hand has on me,
those cursive, kabbalistic strokes by which I learn
you're considering the Müller exercise plan?
Surely it goes without saying that I thought
you'd want no part in it once you discovered
its calisthenics are performed half-naked
in the open air, a detail, no doubt, your civic-
minded doctor means to raise the state
of public health by coaxing the local citizenry
to join in right along with you.
                           Forgive me
if I complain. Between your dissolving marriage
and my engagement postponed for yet another
six months, it seems I'm caught defending myself
at every turn. Just yesterday at lunch,
when I wandered into a café near the armory,
one of the patrons (a man with a beard
like Hindenburg's) tipped back so abruptly
at the sight of me he tumbled over onto the floor.
I took it for granted that the face of a Jew induced
an epileptic fit, so I straightaway turned
and walked back out and lunched on a roll
in my room. The odd thing is, when I first
stepped into the sunlight, it felt good to be alive,
a state of mind I mention because, regardless
of what you think of me, in order to win
your approval I'm prepared to embrace
whatever disabling sorrows life will send my way.
Likewise I now realize why you'll never
be able to return my love: You don't really love
your love for me, and your love for me

doesn't really love you. Accordingly, I fully accept—
indeed, I receive it openheartedly—the little
chastening slap on the hand with which
you closed your latest note: "Surely, Franz,
you'll be able to survive a few more weeks."
I confirm this with my signature.

THE BREAKDOWN

1.

The sun scanned the river with its lidless eye.
Before the heat had choked the saffron fields,
jon boats mulled and idled up the stream.

Mother's blue bedroom steamed behind the blinds.
There, awhile, her heart still murmured
beneath my hand, a bell buoy bobbing on the calms.

2.

I dug in wet sedge for a woodchuck's hole.
The murky, rank, underwater smell
as the hole filled up with mud.

Did she lose herself to the grieving shadows
of the sallow trees? Or did their tracings
unsettle around her? Who was I to say?

3.

And how was I to know? By evening, the crystal
glitter of the water dimmed. She watched
it dim. And egrets lifted languidly

from the hydrophilic glades. On the other bank,
the pulp-mill's whistle sounded the end
for a hip-booted worker on a sawdust pile.

4.

She stood too long on the wooden pier.
Sewer rats scavenged in the sluices,
the radiant moonlight, stars in throngs.

Did she suffer such shining abundance?
The river road down which nothing came?
The empty alabaster palace of the past?

5.

The bedspread swam with splotches of light,
yellow-white on pale-blue. With each breath,
the surface water shuddered from emotion.

I pulled the window blind shut, but the hand
did not loosen in the darkness its grip,
nor the hour forgive her undoing.

from

The Southern Reaches

(1989)

MEMORY

After all the late evenings of that summer
he spent at his grandparents' house, he'd sit outside
on the screened back porch, the homesick
flicker of fireflies in the pines, the scritch of night bugs
loosening into their ambient drone.
It was the hour when a calm settled over the town,
when lamps were lighted and the tide of time
seemed slowed to the breaths he measured it by,
slowed, that is, to the metronomic sough and sigh
of the ventilator he was breathing through.

Often in order to while away the lull before
his grandparents came to carry him in,
he'd count the hours, one by one, back to the hour
when the day began. And in that way
his mind became a kind of closed-off, solitary
room in which he could see played back,
as on a movie screen, small things he'd felt himself
feel that day: the smoke from a coal train
winding through the hills, the cat's milk soured
and yellowing in a bowl; or standing outside
the entry to the downtown five-and-dime,
a girl whose eyes regarded him with that look
of pity and embarrassment he'd often seen
in the faces of those who recognized him.

And just as he would count the hours
back to the hour when the day began, he sometimes

found he couldn't arrest the slowly reversing
stream of time from advancing on its own.
Nor could he always hold in check
the dizzying arc his mind might take
to other, more haphazard things,
things he'd only read about in newspapers
and old magazines, or seen in newsreels
at the Avalon, or overheard in the lowered voices
of adults in another room. And even then,
as if accelerated by an ever-sharpening,
ever-more vivid set of particulars,
yet another stream of images (though now
of things he had no memory of at all)
would skip and flicker across his mind:
a soldier kneeling in the rubble beside
a horse whose belly lay open on the ground;
a man hunched over a wood-spoked wheel
in a frozen ditch in the tundra;
a naked girl whose head was shaved
and who was tied to a post in the middle of a crowd
that milled about her like shoppers.
But from where did all these images come,
if not from him? That was a puzzle
he found impossible to solve, though then
as now it led him to imagine the rising,
nightly concatenation of insects in the trees
was the sound of human memory,
a sound in which nothing is lost
and everything remains, the soft susurrus
of myriad whispered conversations

that after all is said and done
still keep the painful sum of things.

And all the while the boy would sit
motionless in his transport chair, his elbows
on the armrests for balance, the ventilator
filling and guttering out. Too soon, it seemed,
they'd come to take him up to bed. Too soon
he'd have to clear his head for the dreamless sleep
that eluded him more and more these days.
So once they finally settled him in, he found
it helped to pass the time if he'd hum the song
that opened a children's television show
his grandparents, while they had their tea,
would sit him in front of each afternoon at 3:00.

AT THE ALL CLEAR

That early in the morning the village huts
were shuttered in silt. In the headlights' glare,
a field nurse stood with her head in her hands.

A Red Cross truck, its motor running,
sat parked and driverless by the Evangelical
Baptist Church. And all along the beaches,

a wicker surge of cajeput, sea grass,
coconut, palm, and in one small crush
of roofing tiles, a bloated fly-stung

pygmy goat whose head was turned
the wrong way round. As people came down
from the summit, a souring heat

unfocused the waste backed up
in steaming gravel sloughs. Our bungalow
seemed to have been pulleyed up

from a gash in the ground: earth-
spattered, prehistoric, it listed inland
on shaken stilts. And yet, inside,

everything was just as it was before,
the china cabinet still intact, the kitchen table
set for lunch, the shell-and-driftwood mobile

still circling above my made-up bed.
Everything just as it was before. The air
barely rippled through the kitchen curtains

while Mother stood washing the unused plates,
while fire ants beat against the screen
and dropped their sunlit wings on the sill.

AMERICAN AIR BASE AT CHÂTEAUROUX

In the schoolyard's fenced-in football field
    where we'd lunge head and feet first
onto the rocky ground, the crossed chalk line
    electrified our hearts, and no one
much cared for the geopolitical mappings

    in the books we'd stack to mark our goals.
Squared off in teams of threes and fours,
    we grappled with a kind of manhood while
our fathers strafed and lighted up
    "Moscow mockups" in the practice fields,

never far enough away it didn't thunder all day
    in the faces of those who regarded us,
roughed and bloodied and stripped to the waist,
    as conscript godlings marshaled into ranks
to smite the earth and harrow it with salt.

PHOTOGRAPH OF MY FATHER
(Public Gardens, Berlin, 1948)

The sun's suspended like a drop of amber
above the crescent of a colonnade,

and he is standing on a gravel path
between bricked-in flower beds run to seed.

All around, the world's gone gray, like a lapse
in memory. Or like a charcoal sketch

abandoned to a shelf so long ago
that all of its small details—

the young mothers and prams, the pigeons
feeding near the linden trees—time

and circumstance have smudged away. Except
how he's raised his hand in just that way,

as if, from beyond the fading snapshot's frame,
he'd wave to a world that was after he was.

And in that wave, the dull concussions
in the distant hills have started again,

and the empty streets are trembling still
from troop trains passing off to one side

trailing long columns of ash and smoke.

SEASIDE WITH MISSING GODS

The sun-enameled wavelets. A heat that seeps
  from the motel's beach-side redwood deck.
And out beyond the breakers, shore birds
  that in ones and twos freefall as if unwinged by
a scrawl of foil they've been shadowing.
  But everything turns to gospel once you step out
damp and showered from the flower baskets
  beside our door. The late gods gone,
Propertius saw the self-love in a metaphor,
  a likeness that reveals itself to an eye that sees
what can't be seen. Nevertheless,
  he watched his faithless, sunburned Cynthia
rise up like a Nereid from the warm Ionian sea.
  Her hair down, her hair wet, he waited
as she crossed the sand, and then he prayed to god
  she'd dry her swollen breasts on him.

MARRIED LOVE

As they sat and talked beneath the boundary trees
in the abandoned park, neither one mentioning
her husband, or his wife, it seemed as though
their summer shadows had detached themselves
from the confusion of those thousand leaves.
But no more than they could call their shadows
back from the air, could they ignore what they'd undone,
and would undo once more, that afternoon
before giving in to what they knew, had always known.
And yet, in turning away, what they would say
was not that thing, but something else, that mild excuse
that lovers use of how things might have been
had they met somewhere else, or in some better time,
were they less like themselves than what they are.

SKETCHBOOK, PARIS, 9.9.84

As if from the channeled past it came
filling with light the circling paths fronted by plane trees,
pedestaled gods, broad compassing stretches
of shadeless lawn and, here and there, the wrought-
    iron benches,
the wrought-iron chairs from which each moment's
fixed attention strains to disappear. Of course
the mind strains too in its own way to recall
what we ourselves then were, as if things retained
some semblance of the eyes that gazed on them.
And in those eyes three Arab children still huddle around
their mother's skirts, a stone lion leaps across
the fountain spray, and a toque still rests
in the ungloved hand of a Medici who has lost her head
to the charnel waters of a wading pond.

    .

THE ART OF FICTION

It's the way each evening unfolds the same.
The way old men in shirtsleeves come out
to play chess beneath the chestnut trees,
the way shopkeepers linger in their doorways
to talk, while out on the steps young mothers
sit gazing through the empty square
where arm in arm the lovers stroll past,
alone in the privacy of one another's eyes.

And it's the way it all happens so effortlessly.
A little twilight, cook smoke, a *rumba catalana*
from the filling terrace of the Café Noir,
and the bored village boys stop spinning their bicycles
in the sandlot dirt and start hanging around
the fountain and watching. But tonight, it seems,
the woman they are watching they don't understand.
Pacing the walk near the bus station doors,
she smokes and stares and pushes back her hair
in a gesture they find so unlike desire
they can't imagine undressing her there,
for all their remarks and sharp glances.

But suppose the world, as it will at times,
decided tonight to explain such things. Suppose
the woman now hurries across the street
to stop a man just leaving through the café door.
Suppose the man at first draws back
from her, the *rumba catalana* chances to end,

and the noise around them is silenced so
that everyone nearby is drawn nearer.
Then suppose in that moment they could hear
her say, "I've been looking for you.
I thought we could try to make it up somehow,
to make things like they used to be."
Then the silence again. Then the answer:

"I'm sorry," he says, "it's too late now.
And besides, you know, the other woman and all.
You should've thought about that back then."
A pause, but there seems no more to say.
The man walks off through the empty square
and the woman remains alone so long
that the evening finally comes to pass,
the sky goes black, and one by one
bright stars come out that care nothing,
of course, for the sorrow of men's wives,
or for anyone else, for that matter.

HOMAGE TO THE IMPRESSIONIST PAINTERS

In a sight seen once too often, two small boys
with handheld panels are guiding

their nuclear submarines down
beneath the crowded waters of the sailing pond.

Because it's Sunday and early in May
there are countless children, and the gardens

are filled with laughter and shouting
that could almost sound, if you closed your eyes,

like the furious confusions of a battle.
But the bordering roses are sorbet pinks,

the leaves of the lilac so palely green
they seem formed from seawater and plankton.

And down the long allées of pollarded trees
the yoked rental ponies are painted with a shade

that increases their shyness and importance.
A unicyclist turning figure eights in the sand,

the usual circle of men playing *boules*,
and a group of white-frocked teenage girls—

apprentice surgeons? meat-market clerks?—
with flecks of blood high up on their sleeves.

Out in a glade cordoned off with chain
(like Paradise, it's not to walk on but there

to see) a woman has spread a blue bed sheet
and placed a rock at each end. She smiles

at the world from her place in the world,
and she isn't disturbed, nor should she be,

by the sudden, ecstatic cry that says: Open
your eyes, the sky's overhead, treetops

are swimming through the warm spring air,
and the moment of death is rising in the pond

where all is lovely, and crazy, and contrived.

THE ENORMOUS AQUARIUM OF MARCEL PROUST

All morning long from inside the lobby
of the Grand Hotel, the sun-bleached arras
of the seascape hung suspended within
the sky-high mullioned window's frame.
And it was only at widening intervals,
as cards were shuffled and dealt around the fours,
that one of the players, suppressing
a barely audible yawn or marking the arrival
of some new guest, would rouse himself
to glance outside at an occasional sail
on the horizon. So, too, the afternoon hours,
immutable and bland, would silver the glass
that more and more, as the day declined,
came to seem like mirrors in which you look
and find a face so pale, so drained of all
deliberate care, you politely bow and avert
your eyes.
   For all those mute concessions,
it seemed the day hadn't yet begun
until the cooling offshore breeze arose
to portion out shadow and reduce the sun
to a pomegranate stain that thinned to shimmer
under indigo. It followed then, by the sweep
of some imaginary hand, that an undulant stream
of electric light poured from the various
pendants and sconces and high-tiered
Flemish chandeliers, so the hotel seemed,
in the privacy of its marine-like glow,

like an enormous aquarium the soughing sea
filled up by night and drained by day.

Submerged as they were in their element,
the residents hardly noticed when the fishermen's
and the tradesmen's families, clustering
invisibly in the outer dark, would sometimes
come and press their faces against the glass.
For what alien creatures floated past
on those golden eddies of unrippling light:
there, a cavalry officer, his organdy plume
like the cursive fin of an emperor fish;
there, an octogenarian Chevalier whose mien
the years had fashioned in the bourns
of Faubourg Saint-Germain; or there,
high-born and aloof, the dowager Duchess,
her powdered jaws closing on a morsel of food
like some primitive shellfish closing
on a spore.
            And the question now looming
in the outside air was how the polished
discretions of the glass could hold
a world so vastly different from the poor,
a world where charmeuse and sable,
grosgrain and emerald and a Samarkand
silk beribboned spray of egret feathers
tied to the braid of a young girl's hair
could speak of a life so far beyond the reach
of even their most unheard of dreams.
It was, of course, only a matter of time before
such passing interest came to pass, before

the families finally turned away from what they saw
to what they were. The unhoused dark
now set the scene, the sea air bore the scent
of pine from the wooded bluffs, and beneath
a moon as round as an eye
they made their way down the quiet streets
like some ancient, imperishable tribe.

from

The City of Women

(1994)

The storybook closed. The rocking stopped.
The moment of saying carrying on in a long
duologue of silence. Yet while she throned
among her secret thoughts, some rooted,

half-formed memory poured from the pleated
muslin of her skirts. And all that endless afternoon,
the fan's rotation sweeping past in muffled,
quickly taken breaths. A stifled sob?

Some ghost out stalking a necropolis?
Or sleep descending (though slower now
that the war is over and her loss undone)
with the sudden eloquence of speechlessness.

~

She is seated somewhere—I can't recall where
exactly now—the young Algerian shop clerk
from a bookstore Mother frequented then.
She is seated alone—in a café, let's say—
looking out onto the crowded square,
a mingling fretwork of pushcarts, string bags,
makeshift stalls, an acrid smell off the *pissoirs*,
and the dizzying zigzag horseflies make
in the airless crush of those afternoons.

But all the heaped activity out of which
I've just caught sight of her seems not to break
upon the stillness that surrounds her where
she's lifting a spoon to sip some chocolate
from a steaming bowl. And though it had rained
earlier, the sun is out, the sun's reflected off
the window she sits staring from,
so that her image deepens behind the pane,
advances as if out of flame, and then recedes again
into a glassy incandescence our desolate world
would crisscross for a moment before the next
cloud came and shadowed her back,
as in the fade-out of a movie screen.

This is a picture I've kept for thirty years,
it's always there, in a silence of which
I've never spoken, a suspension bridge
across that time which in some ways

does not exist, will never exist, the story
of my life in love, the buried life I know little about,
perhaps know nothing at all. But picking my way
through the marketplace that afternoon
on my mother's arm, I've been in love for days,
for weeks, though foolish as this may sound,
I didn't know that I was until, figured as she is
in the fired, unapproachable glare of the windowpane,
she seems so beautiful she frightens me.

≈

Already in advance our lives owe something to those moments. An induction. A knowledge. An unlikeness between ourselves (before) and our-selves (thereafter). And a barely perceptible disharmony with all of our surroundings, as though the world had just contracted around a newly engendered set of senses. As though the world in vast, incalculable ways had put a DIFFERENT FACE ON THINGS.

That much we realize even then.

~

My name, L. tells me, is really Marianne. There was a boy she'd known in boarding school, the best friend of a boyfriend she'd been seeing in those days. A boy who'd occasionally gone out with them, who rarely paid her any attention, and who, for some reason, could never recall her name. One day she decided she'd had enough, and while her boyfriend was gone she told him so.

The boy was crushed. Embarrassed. He said he was sorry. He said it was because she didn't *seem* like a Marianne, it just didn't suit her, not *that* name. It's the name, that's all, the *name*. It was then she realized it was shyness not indifference that had made him so aloof; she realized, as well, that in his way he'd cared for her, cared deeply, perhaps, through all those weeks he'd been with them. He said he was sorry again and again, and while he was apologizing he began to cry, not making much noise, just tears and a look resembling grief. After that he stopped coming around. He was a good friend for my boyfriend, she says, but we never saw him again.

The loss in her voice awakens in me a loss as well. So because of him you changed your name? Oh, come on, she says (though she's faraway now), let's not go into that. I was nineteen at the time and didn't much care for the name myself. Who knows why we do what we did back then.

~

I never tried to untangle her stories, to puzzle out their facts and illusions, for I felt I was somehow in sympathy, even at times in complicity, with what I believed her motive was: A desire to disguise the flesh in words, the words themselves a costume for the self we'd have the other love.

And, in truth, I couldn't imagine calling her Marianne.

~

A busy corner. A crush of people crossing
the street. People waiting for buses, loitering
in doorways, staring from half-open windows.
And a woman of forty or forty-five (she's wearing
a light-blue cashmere suit) pacing the block
between a kiosk and a newspaper stand.
I have never seen this woman before.
I will never see her again. Except that way.
Pacing. Watching. Waiting for someone
who never comes. A San Francisco street corner.
A warm spring morning in May of 1972.

~

I'd met Zoë only weeks before—she'd moved to Paris from Amsterdam and now worked as an *au pair*—and one afternoon while we're having coffee, she asked me to tell her a story, about anything that I pleased. Because I couldn't think of anything else, I told her about a little-known section of the city, three or four blocks near St.-Germain—had she been there yet?—where a number of young designers had recently set up shops.

Their boutiques are sparsely furnished, and because most of the designers are still quite poor, they exhibit only a handful of garments, a dozen or so trademark dresses, a smaller number of jackets and tops, a scattering of knits and scarves.

So that men can shop for their wives or lovers, each boutique has on hand an assistant who doubles as a model. Most shops, comprised of a single well-lit room, have no dressing area per se, so normally the assistant changes behind a broad swatch of material strung straight out from the wall. The curtain is largely ceremonial, for once the clothes are selected the designer begins to describe such things as fabrics, falls, the flares of the dress, and the curtain is normally swept aside to illustrate those details.

When the man accompanies a wife or lover, the custom is slightly altered since, most times, she'll try on the clothes herself. The assistant then fills the alternate role of lady-in-waiting, helping the woman in and out of her things while the designer, having once again swept the curtain aside, describes the garments as before.

When I finished my story, I told her one day I'd like to take her to visit those shops, to watch her pick out clothes, to watch her dressed and undressed in turn by the shop assistant's capable hands. Tell me more, she said, about what you'd like to do. But there was nothing more I could think to tell.

Weeks later—we still weren't lovers—she invited me to the address of a woman who, while traveling, had hired her to keep her flat. As soon as I came in, Zoë led me into a bedroom where the shutters were open to the evening air. There were two or three vases of flowers, candles set out here and there, and draped over a bureau against the wall, numerous articles of the owner's clothes.

She motioned for me to sit on the bed, and then, very slowly, without saying a word, she removed her loose unwaisted dress and began to try on clothes. Though not, I imagined, in the manner of a wife or lover. She dressed, instead, with the slightly studied, businesslike air of one of the shop assistants. She dressed, as it were, ANONYMOUSLY, and rarely even looked my way, though her skin gave off the faintest scent of opium, a fragrance she'd attempted to cover over with a drop of vanilla behind each ear.

~

My mother's family was Southern, affluent, aristocratic. My father's, working-class, immigrant, resettled near the hop fields in northern California. When they met in 1942, at the height of the war, they were both, so to speak, in disguise, my mother in the somber, pinstriped outfit of the volunteers at the USO, my father in the full military splendor of an Air Corps pilot on R & R.

In that sense, the haste of their wedding was a crisis, and their marriage an ongoing version of the historical struggle between social and economic classes. Except they both subscribed to the same ideological principles: this was always a matter of REGRET, that of BLAME, the other of MAKING AMENDS.

~

Where to begin? My earliest memory is dipped
in an acid of ammonia and sweat. An enamel box
with large, weirdly illuminated numerals,
and a sweltering room where the curtains billow
outside in on a man and woman, mid-embrace,
who've just stopped dancing to stare at me
with a barely concealed displeasure. But then,
kneeling down in front of me, the woman smiles
and, in a voice just slightly sweeter than she is,
says "Now we play some hide-and-seek." A damp
bandana drawn from around her braided hair
(its warm compress against my eyes) is tied
in a knot at the back of my head. A door clicks shut,
locks—from the caustic fumes, I can tell
it's the cleaning closet I'm in—and a faraway
music washes over a second sound, like an *O*
that's muffled repeatedly until it gutters
in a groan. I don't dare move or say a word.
I don't dare trouble the spawn of light motes
floating in the dark behind my lids, each one
a face I search until a hush pours over me,
prayer-like and cool. When I come to,
the blindfold's off, the man is gone, and in yet
another tone of voice—throaty, close up,
edged with rum—she tells me he is hiding now,
"And he can see you though you can't see him."
The threat works. From that moment on I'm aware
of him, his eyes on me, his face somewhere

concealed behind the rictus of a grin. I'm far
too frightened to tell anyone, and it's only years later
that Mother recalls the curtained windows
(and the Blaupunkt radio) of our two-room house
on the coast of Bermuda. And the Lancashire maid,
discharged early for showing up drunk,
who had looked after me when I was five.

~

L. and I are sitting outside in early June.
She has kicked off her sandals. Her hair
is down and swept back off her shoulders.
The fireflies have found enough of a dark
against which to strike their phosphor. A faint,
lemon-scented candle. Castor and Pollux
struggling to rise through the still re-needling
cypress trees. And out of the coalescing dark,
she asks the question all lovers ask: What
in me first attracted you? By the time I answer,
she has leaned back heavily into her chair
and closed her eyes, though I can't tell
if it's from boredom, anger, amusement or,
as I choose to think (for it's what in her
first attracted me), her brutal cinematic ways.

~

One evening in spring I take Zoë out to a magic show on the
Rue Mouffetard. It begins with an array of dove pans, card tricks,
body illusions, and ends with a version of "The Radium Girl,"
a trick in which the female assistant is bound in chain and laid
in a long, coffin-shaped box. A panel is secured to the top of
the box and, with great fanfare, the magician then proceeds to
drive a series of glittering swords every which way through the
polished wood. Each time he does, Zoë draws a sudden intake of
breath—not as in wonder, but in a kind of reflexive physical pain.

Later that night when we make love, I have the sense she sees
me trying to reenact the violence of the magic show. Each time
I enter her, the same gasp I'd heard before.

In the morning, however, it's gone:

~

Do this, she says, and this. I make
as if to do what she says, but already
she's there before me. Her eyes
shut, Let me do it. Do that, she says,
and she does. And the moan, as of
a pain withdrawn, a suspiration,
a letting go:

an emptying vessel

of thought and desire.

~

She had the watchful, pale, water-colored eyes her doctor called "light-sensitive," though she was someone who seemed to take great pleasure in the play of light on surfaces: the needlepoint glitter of pines at dawn, a sun-struck pane of window glass, the sparkle of pond ice, the backlit coruscations of a storm . . . I wonder now if it's that my father was thinking of:

Christmas morning at my mother's parents' baronial house. Everyone dressed in Sunday clothes, each of us presented with a package while the others sit and watch. No one really wants to go next, and it's Mother's turn, my father's gift whose sleight-of-hand has thoroughly fooled us all. Slowly, almost tenderly, she removes the wrapping from what we've guessed is a bottle of champagne. Only it isn't champagne at all, but a dummy bottle from which she draws—astonished BEYOND THE REACH OF WORDS—a dress of glittering, gold lamé, like an overflow of warm champagne.

The kids break into loud applause, though it's Grandfather she is turning to, as if into the weird distortions of a funhouse mirror, when she rises to say, "I couldn't possibly anywhere ever wear anything even remotely like this."

And that is that. My father dumbstruck. Mother humiliated. Grandfather apparently satisfied.

~

Early morning, a woman sits up in bed
with a cup of coffee and an ashtray in her lap,
though she isn't smoking and the coffee
has long since cooled. For the last two months
she and her husband have slept in separate rooms,
and now, by habit, it's decided this room
is "hers." Beyond the window, a vesper sparrow
is tearing away at the wildly overgrown
lantana bush, stabbing at its inky, blue-black berries,
some of which fall onto the window ledge
already badly stained. Before entering her room
(he's dressed for work and probably in a hurry),
her husband pauses and shuffles his feet
as though wiping his shoes on a mat.
At the sound this makes, she looks up at him
undisturbed, and so manages once more
to turn a loss into the SEMBLANCE OF A LOSS.

~

My neighbor is drunk. He has broken his hand.
He has run out into the front yard yelling,
My wife's a fucking cocksucking whore!
Months later, the smell of autumn leaf fires in the air,
I see the two of them, arm in arm, walking home
from the grocery store. And I'm deeply moved
by the resilience, by the unfathomable mystery
of the human heart. And then, almost instantly
(and with equal force), by its credulity,
its cowardice, its desperate fear of being alone.

~

L. arose one morning and began to wash
the floors and windows in all the rooms
of our rented house. It took her late
into the afternoon, and when she finished
she sat in a chair and wept out loud
because, as she said, I hadn't even tried to stop her.
Later that night she described to me
how accustomed she'd grown to certain fears.
When I was a child I'd wake up in a strange bed
and scream. Now I wake up time and again
and have learned to accept it passively.

~

And again she's saying, *This can't go on.* And again she's saying it reasonably, though we both know what she means: *What's going on, what keeps going on, what will go on no matter what we do,* is the very thing that *can't go on.* I have no response. We've been through this, this "in between," a hundred times before, and once she sees there's nothing left, she says to me, with a contempt that must've surprised even her, *You look like someone who's forgotten to suffer.*

~

—I can hardly pretend to forgive you for being who—or what—you are.

—First you say practically nothing and then immediately you take it back.

—After all you've said I feel the same as I did before (her gaze turned toward the ground).

—It's as if you've stopped "listening" or "not listening" and started "unlistening" to everything I say.

—I never imagined it would be like this. (Pause) *I never imagined it otherwise.*

—And then you'll say, So how do you feel, and for hours after I'll find myself at a loss for words.

—It's like being pregnant all over again, though I can't tell if I'm heavy with the past or big with the future.

Giving and forgiving, saying and unsaying, thus we'd seem to arrive at periods that were wholly outside time. Ended, always, by one or the other relenting, just *saying the word*, though THE WORD was random and likewise about purely external things. This, perhaps, is the enduring part of the story: those anticipated, hence inevitable endings. And the illusion, the towering LITERARY illusion, that we somehow brought them on ourselves.

~

Zoë decides we shouldn't see each other, though why that is she regards as beside the point: *It just doesn't feel like it used to feel.*

Months pass without a word, and then one day she invites me to meet her in a restaurant. The first thing she talks about is "the sex," how she misses *that* but not the *other.* Oddly enough, I know what she means. In fact, I can see in all those *other* respects how tiresome our feelings had grown. Still, she wonders, why not act on the one and not the other. Even now, sitting here, divided by a table in the Bal Musette—why not?

As she continues talking, I'm reminded again of how slender her wrists are, how pale, almost translucent her skin, how urgent the voice which gathers and releases all the unloosed ardor of her words.

~

After the divorce my mother moved, as she liked to say, "to a town in another time zone." A deliberate period of mourning followed. And then:

She learned to pump her own gas, replace the fuses in a circuit box, sketch out a weekly budget plan. Her love of gardening was now dismissed as something for which she had no time. In less than a year she stopped ending her letters: "I hope all of you are better off than I am."

While she became more cautious about certain things—like how much cash she carried in her purse—she also seemed to lose her fear of going out alone. Squinting unnaturally (because she's just come out of a matinee?), she's leaning against a movie marquee for *The Diary of a Country Priest.* It's not clear who has taken the picture, and for one childishly painful moment I imagine her stopping a stranger on the street. Someone completely unaware of the enormous effort it took for her— betrayed by the glare—to present herself AT EASE.

But why *had* she chosen to be pictured that way? Surely, "at this distance from the marriage," Bresson's film was intended as a joke. Its austere evocation of the religious life, its useless young priest who finds that life, in any case, so spiritually unrewarding. Or was it, like a joke, meant to convey a message she appeared on the surface to ridicule? The message: Don't pity me.

~

How often these days, struggling to recall some incident or other, I'm struck by a feeling of sifting through ash; and the adult fantasy (tinged with dread) that who we are is composed of what, perhaps only what, we can never reclaim from the rubble. Then, as well, there are certain moments that advance in time:

~

When they'd argue, I'd grow calm. When they didn't speak, I'd grow talkative. A feeling of well-being, like taking a breath, releasing.

*

A young married couple from out of town struggling together— because they just can't give up holding hands—to open the heavy cathedral doors.

*

A woman who, to keep from crying, steps into a shop selling artificial limbs.

*

Somewhere in the mysterious turnings of sleep, her asking her father for a glass of milk.

*

My mother in a sundress on the first day of spring, though it's raining heavily and cold outside.

*

In the middle of the night, the light from their bedroom shining in the garden.

*

The smell of salt grass off Half Moon Bay.

*

A bouquet of flowers (alyssum, sweet William, tea roses, fern) left behind on the concrete rail of the sailing pond, Luxembourg Gardens, Paris, 1984.

*

The SHARED EMOTION of a radio song.

*

The MOMENTARY HAPPINESS in a stranger's voice.

*

L. pausing to stare at a bright contrail swept by high, stratospheric winds on an evening walk in July.

from

The Pilot Star Elegies

(1999)

THE STORY

in memory of M. L. Rosenthal

What are we to make of this story? This is,
after all, the twentieth century, and if any age ever
showed a lack of faith in, among other things,
the structures of a story, surely it must be ours.
It arrived by accident in the afternoon mail
from a secondhand bookshop in London, a misdirected
copy sent instead of the order I had placed
for an out-of-print book by a friend. My friend
who'd retired the year before was living abroad
at the time, and his lifelong study of the Hebrew elegy
was no doubt mailed to someone waiting, expecting
to receive a copy of the book that I received,
Hasidic Tales of the Holocaust. A mistake perhaps
explainable in any number of ways, including
the one my friend had guessed: "Some closet
anti-Semitic clerk who finds such jokes can pass the day."
Nevertheless, in my own stubbornly secular way,
I believe those books that we need most
choose us and not the other way around,
so I opened the book right then and read,
at the kitchen table, in a small, square panel
of sunlight framing the closely printed page,
the first of those tales the author recorded
just as she had heard them reported to her.

How late in the middle of a frozen night
in the Janowska road camp, upper Ukraine,
a voice on the speakers had crackled through,

"You will evacuate the barracks immediately
and report to the field by the vacant lot." In the frantic
confusion that followed, the shouted names
of relatives and friends filled the air, and like
a broken vessel the barracks poured out
in the direction of the field by the vacant lot.
Huddled together against the cold, the prisoners
slowly began to make out, at a distance beyond them
in the treeless dark, two wide and freshly dug pits.
Once more, the voice on the speakers
crackled through, "All of you who value
your miserable lives must jump over one of the pits
and land on the other side. For those who fail
there's a surprise in store." And then, as a child
imitates machine gun sounds, *rata-tat-tat*
trailed off into wild, uproarious laughter.

Among the thousands of Jews in the field that night
was the Rabbi of Bluzhov standing with a friend,
a freethinker from Poland he'd met in the camp.
"Rebbe," the friend said, "forgive me, but all our attempts
to jump over the pits are in vain. At best, we'll only
lighten the spirits of the S.S. and those pig-hearted
Ukrainian collaborators. It's just as well that we sit
and wait for the bullets that will end our suffering."
"My friend," said the rabbi, turning in the direction
of the open earth, "man must obey the will of God.
If heaven has decreed that pits will be dug
and we will be commanded to jump, then pits will be dug,
and jump we must. And if, God forbid, we fail

and fall into those pits, then we will only reach
the World of Truth a little sooner than we thought."

The rabbi and his friend were nearing the pits
which were rapidly filling with bodies and,
now that the dark was beginning to lift, looked
a good deal wider than they'd first appeared.
The rabbi looked down at his feet, the bandaged feet
of a sixty-three-year-old Jew wracked by starvation
and disease. He looked at his friend, a skeleton
with a burning stare. When they reached the edge,
the rabbi closed his eyes and said, "We are jumping!"
And when he opened his eyes, he and his friend
were standing together on the other side.
With sudden, unexpected tears (he wouldn't
have believed he had more tears) the friend cried out,
"We're here! We're here! We made it, Rebbe!
But how? What did you do? How did you do it?"
"I was holding on to the coattails of my father,"
he said. And then, looking into the eyes of his
Polish friend, "But how did you make it over as well?"
"I was holding on to you," the friend replied.
And neither was sure which was the more miraculous.
And neither was sure they'd even survived
as anything more than the insane and unvarying wish
of two men leaping headlong into a pit.

When I closed the book, the small, square
panel of sunlight had shifted a little to my left
so that part of it still leveled across the tabletop

while the other part lay, halved and unbroken,
on the kitchen floor. So far as I could tell,
nothing much had changed in the world,
perhaps nothing at all had changed in me.
My wife came home a little while later and,
as usual, I went off to collect our sons from school.
And that was that. A few years passed,
the afternoon seemed to recede in time,
and I didn't really think about it much anymore.
But this morning at breakfast a letter arrived
informing me that my friend had died. And suddenly
it all came back again, as clear to me now as it was
that day, the story of two men huddled together
at the edge of a pit, the *rata-tat-tat*, and that small,
square panel of sunlight sliding across the printed page.

I

from OF HALOES & SAINTLY ASPECTS

1. Sea Turtle

Out of a ripple in the sea grass,
two unhoused fiddler crabs
sidestep past the almost-dead

hawksbill turtle turned over
on the beach and left there staked
with a length of broomstick

and baling wire. The squared,
inquiring head upstraining,
the plastron split, and the sun-

dazed eyes that will not weep
for such incongruities
as these: faced into the current

of an onshore breeze,
the scalding hollow of its carapace
tightens around the plum-

size heart. Anchored
to the earth it left behind, it oars
the deep, inverted sea

and labors toward it still,
its little destiny undisturbed by acts
of forgiveness or contrition.

2. Sarah

Car lights like lanterns in the predawn dark.
The smell of cocoa from a thermos cup.
A light summer shower that comes and goes
against the wipers' fan-shapes snapping closed.

Already my mother is slipping downward
into sleep, a hushed night music
on the radio. She dreams. And wakes.
But what has frightened her?

The sudden vibration of the metal bridge?
The glare? "We're there now, Sarah,"
her father says, as if all of this,
still vaguely seen, has happened before:

the guard politely nodding as they pass;
the space that opens into her each time
they brake to turn onto the tree-lined drive
of the asylum in Staunton, Virginia. Inside,

dressed and attended by a wardroom nurse,
her mother's preparing to meet her guests
(as was her rule) with that look of polite
forbearance she'd long ago been widowed to.

3. Minnows

The river, while it runs the gamut of all
lowered eyes gathered on the sandbar, whirlpools
in around a snagged tree limb trailing
the red flag of the drowned girl's blouse.

Just moments before that moment, she'd wrestled
with her brothers while her father spilled
a dipnet full of minnows in a Mason jar,
and now the jar, the net, the flattened reeds

beside their fishing poles, remain as they
could not help but remain; now, with a swift,
almost unconscious purpose such daily rituals
compose in time, the coptered-in reporter

from the *Post Dispatch* opens up his notebook
and tries again to get it down in just that way:
the sloped sand shelf, the trailing blouse,
the minnows blindly bumping at the glass.

5. Dalai Lama

From between the pages of a 1968 junk store copy
of D'Aulaire's *Norse Gods and Giants*,
the five clean-cut crenellate petals of a flower

almost alchemical in its papery likeness
to what it was, a sign conspired to preserve
some tremor in an adolescent heart,

to round out phyla in a science notebook
kept for school, or perhaps, in fear, to summon
the wandering Valkyries whose muraled lives

are marked for good by the cinnabar
leached off its cells. A dead metaphor
carrying on long past its paradigm

of human need, it continues into the future
freed of our small demands on it,
like the exiled Tibetan god-king blessed
with the common sense to survive himself.

SPRING ELEGY

for a student of mine, Frank Vincent,
who died of AIDS, 3.17.97

All morning in class that hollow feeling of how little
we've been left to say; and then, a few hours later
while I'm downstairs checking the afternoon mail,
someone comes in and lays out neatly on my office desk
a black-and-white photograph, a sprig of forsythia,
and a tenth share of his ashes in a smoked glass vial.

NOCTURNES

1.

Do you have the poems of Han-shan in your house?
Han-shan asks at the end of his poem. Cold mountain.
Ice flowers on the windowpane. Exhausted from sledding
all afternoon, the boys have dragged their sleeping bags out
in front of the fire, Lynne under blankets beside them.
Having earlier drawn the shortest length of broomstraw,
I've been sitting up reading by lantern light
these words that no one will believe. Now, past midnight,
rising to bank up hardwood for that slow burn through
till morning, I suddenly recall my childhood wish
to live invisibly, to close my eyes and not be seen.
A fear of death? I think perhaps the opposite: a desire
to escape the life of facts. A thousand, ten thousand years,
do you recognize me, air, where once I wandered?

2.

We're cleaning up after the guests have gone,
the two of us drying the last of the dishes,
a little light-headed from all of the wine,
a little undone by that touch of melancholy
that lingers in the air after parties these days.
Then somehow or other it comes around
I ask about him, who he was, and how was it
it had happened. But there's not that much
she remembers, truly, there's scarcely anything
at all. Oh, his eyes perhaps. And then, now

that she thinks about it, wasn't it his first time
as well? Yes, his eyes, she remembers, his eyes,
when he entered her, his eyes were the same
uncomplicated blue of borage or deep water.

3.

Late August, and once again the frail moon's
launched like an air balloon off the flat-roofed
campus bookstore. Once again, the night watch
takes his cake and coffee on the concrete bench
beyond my door. The twelve taped chimes
of the clock tower bell, the twelve short echoes
that follow. A silence, then, through the indrawn
hush of the library doors, two exhausted students,
stunned to reenter the womb-weight of the humid air,
linger a moment to say goodbye before lugging
their heavy backpacks off in opposite directions.
How many years will this scene go on repeating itself?
How many years before one of them takes
the other's hand, and the poem is brought to an end?

II

from ELEGY FOR MY SISTER

We ought to say a feeling of *and*, a feeling of *if*, a feeling of *but*,
a feeling of *by*, quite as readily as we say a feeling of *blue* or a
feeling of *cold*. Yet we do not; so inveterate has our habit become
of recognizing the existence of the substantive parts alone, that
language almost refuses to lend itself to any other use.

—WILLIAM JAMES,
The Principles of Psychology

A vague, faintly outlined idea. . . . Then from the furthest reaches
of the self, in sonorous transfiguration, may be heard a noise, a
sound, a tonality which by its very insistence must either paralyze
us forever or preserve our life anew.

—E. M. CIORAN,
The Temptation to Exist

In the daylight she sat in the rocking chair on the terrace. The
moving crowns of the pine trees were reflected on the window
behind her. She began to rock; she raised her arms. She was lightly
dressed, with no blanket on her knees.

—PETER HANDKE,
The Left-Handed Woman

1.

Sketchbooks. Night fires. Aesop and Grimm.
An electric model of the Lipizzaner stallions
circling each other in her darkened room.
Her vine-borne flowering marginalia, flowering now
in the ever-widening margins of memory.
The up-early privacy of a house at dawn
and a jigsaw puzzle, disarranged, arranging
(the quick bird-movement of her slender hands)
into evergreen leaves on a holly tree.
The window she'd look in each time we'd pass
the Home for Retarded Children.
My feeling (no doubt hopelessly tinged
with how, were she here, her looks alone
would resist my attempts to say these things)
that all of this was already lost even then.
The Palace of Nowhere. L'Hôtel de Dream.

2.

    . . . And so it is I begin this now
a week after my sister's suicide, for I can already
feel her slipping beyond the reach of words,
and words like bread crumbs trailed behind her
on the forest floor are all that's left to lead her back
through the sunless weathers of the afterworld.
But I begin this for another reason as well,
a more urgent and perhaps more selfish reason,
to answer that question which day by day
I fear I'm growing less able to answer: Who was she
whose death now made her a stranger to me?
As though the problem were not that she had died,
and how was I to mourn her, but that some
stalled memory now kept her from existing,
that she could only begin to exist, to take
her place in the future, when all of our presuppositions
about her, all of those things that identified
the woman we'd buried, were finally swept aside.
As though the time of her being remained,
as yet, a distant premonition within us.

4.

Though I don't recall her mentioning God—
and though she shrank from personal pieties
of whatever sort—her power over others,
if not herself, seemed to come from
the inward certainty of those who believe
they're blessed by their misfortunes.
But there was always something in the way
she chose to present herself to the world—
the secondhand plaid and floral skirts,
the thrift store jewelry, the chewed down,
brightly polished nails—which somehow lightened
that first impression. Is it possible that,
like those mongrel dogs that often appear
in seventeenth-century religious paintings,
her appearance was arranged to counter the effect
of some otherwise unabated spiritual yearning?
That this was simply another way
she fought the ascendancy of her own soul?

5.

(State Hospital, Nashville, 1979)

Behind the fretted network of a cast-iron grille
she stood untouched by the holiday lights
strung haphazard in Admissions,
a ticked synaptic flicker, first in amethyst,
then in flame. Convalescent, bloodshot,
unreachable, fifteen years ago she watched
those thermostatic light motes flare and glaze
the double windowpanes. And now,
beside a tray of stubbed-out cigarette ends,
she takes a hand mirror and looks again
past that figure drawn up suddenly,
as through a wide theoptic eye, at that something
going on inside in ways the shocked brain's
weird illogic strains to accelerate and shelter.

6.

She was born *Sarah Gossett Ballenger,*
Sarah our mother's proper name, Gossett our mother's
family name, Ballenger the name of her father.
Following our mother's second marriage,
her name was changed to *Sarah Ballenger Santos,*
and when she herself got married, she became
Sarah Ballenger Santos Knoeppel. After her divorce,
she changed her name to *Sarah Beth Ballenger,*
though *Beth* was chosen simply because
she liked its "sound," and because, for once,
she'd felt entitled to name herself.
Following a stillbirth in the twelfth year
of her marriage, she instructed her daughters
to refer to her as *Mimi*—not *Mommy,* not *Mother,*
not *Mom.* At some point after she left home
(she was sixteen or seventeen at the time),
she changed the spelling of her familiar name
from *Sally* to *Salley,* and of her proper name
from *Sarah* to *Sara,* though here, too, the reasons
she gave were largely a matter of taste:
she just found those spellings more "personal."
Thus all her life she felt her name
referred to a self she hardly knew, a self
which sought to separate her from who she was.
Thus all her life she was never quite sure
who it was people summoned whenever they called her

by her name. And, more specifically,
she was never quite sure they recognized her
when, and if, she responded. As she put it,
at various periods in her life she'd "lent" herself
to particular names, only to reclaim herself
in time, only to "suppose" all over again.

7.

My sister left no note behind. This was reason enough for some in the family to believe her death an accident, not a willful act, not a suicide. In the days before the funeral, my mother was given to saying to those who called on the phone, "She just died, that's all." But saying it with a tone of besieged impatience, so as to cut off further questioning.

Her appearance in the casket had a symbolic meaning perhaps lost to anyone outside the family. The clothes my mother had chosen for her recalled that time, twenty years earlier, when she'd struggled for months to impersonate the life of an "ordinary" person. A black knit sweater with roses embroidered across the chest. A full frill collar. A "virginity pin." A knee-length, wine-colored, lamb's-wool skirt.

Her hands were folded *peacefully* on her chest; her nails were done up *tastefully*; her head was cushioned on a silken pillow in an attitude of *calm repose*. Preparations meant, not to recall her "as she was in life," but to bestow on her the equanimity (or perhaps, in truth, the respectability) her life in our eyes had always lacked.

9.

As a rule, my sister didn't care for social gatherings,
though when she went she carried away
a palpable feeling of euphoria. This wasn't, however,
the euphoria of "a good time," but of someone
who'd managed to pass unseen through the field
of other people's stares. In this and other respects,
she reminded me of those blue translucent birds
("so the hawks can't see them against the sky")
Marlon Brando describes in *The Fugitive Kind*.
Those legless birds that "don't belong no place
at all," and so stay on the wing until they die.

10.

(Vanderbilt University Hospital, 1983)

She woke near ten and once again she found
the blue-beating line of light mounting like a migraine
on the plasticine. A small pot of pink impatiens,
her lamplit, high-strung folding bed like a river-
rounded island city against which the darkness
lapped and rose. And then the full bodyweight of it,
the pinprick of consciousness breaking on the skin.

11.

Because of her "instability" doctors were reluctant
to write her prescriptions, though she was very adept
at describing symptoms which called for the drugs
she wanted. She was also doggedly insistent.
One physician I telephoned defended his decision
by explaining how, during one of her many
unscheduled visits, she'd remained in his office
refusing to leave until he'd written her a scrip
for sleeping pills. To be "cautious," he said,
he'd written it for only "half the normal number."
Which perhaps explains why, on the floor beside her bed,
we found empty vials for four different drugs,
each prescribed by a different doctor—meprobamate,
propoxyphene, amitriptyline, carisoprodol—
a lethal combination of soma compounds, pain pills,
tension relievers, and triptans. Clearly, killing herself
required the same cunning, the same unspoken
complicity of others, that she'd needed to stay alive.

12.

Several weeks after the funeral, while watching
a home movie of my niece's wedding, I feel suddenly
and hopelessly exposed when the camera pans past
my sister seated in one of the folding chairs.
But what guilt, or sadness, was I hiding from?
The knowledge that nothing I'd done had helped?
The fear that I'd done nothing at all? That brief
but nonetheless clear sensation, when the phone call came,
that it was finally over with, finished and done?
This evening, while I was downstairs working
at the kitchen table, I could hear my wife scolding our son
for marking with crayons on the bedroom wall.
"Aren't you ashamed of yourself?" she asked him.
And I couldn't help thinking, "Yes, I am."

16.

We stood at the back gate where the other patients
were less likely to wander wide-eyed past the orderlies.
And in the check station's neutral stump of shade,
about to say goodbye, she came down suddenly
from her high room, focused, then let go a web
of Seconal from her frazzled hair. "Sometimes I feel
like a balloon blown up well beyond its limit."
A figure of speech she stepped back from
and seemed to ponder from afar, as if, by chance,
she'd managed at last to describe herself to herself.

20.

She was someone about whom people remarked:
She never seemed to find a life for herself. Or:
Her life was the story of a long collapse, its end
a dark, unlucky star she'd clung to hopefully,
for better or worse. Shortly after her death,
we found in her closet a large, taped-up
cardboard box of skincare products and tools—
renewal serums, a camouflage brush, eyeliners,
bronzers, exfoliates, scrubs. Many of them
had never been opened, still others had barely
been used. Sorting through the contents
it occurred to me that the box contained some version
of herself she'd never had the chance to become.
Sorting through the contents it occurred to me:
She once was becoming; she ceased to become.

21.

Is it inconceivable (I suspect this question haunts
us all) that all her life she was misunderstood?
That we spoke a language which for whatever reasons
she herself had never learned? That all her attempts
to draw us in only further served to hold us apart?
That she'd had good reason to defend as true
what we'd perceived as utterly false? That what
she'd said in love or affection we heard
as confusion, anger, fear? Of course, these questions
have no beginning or end and like posterity
they fuel themselves on a bottomless human vanity:
the illusion that we can "know" someone.
And yet, not to go on asking questions is to follow
that line through time and space that leads us
to experience her death—conclusively? nostalgically?
consolingly?—as "the final pages of a novel."
And how could she ever forgive us that?

23.

A dream I started having several weeks ago.
As in the newsreel of some dignitary-or-other
arriving in a foreign country, she descends the stairs
from an airplane cabin, and with each step
her face grows steadily younger and more beautiful,
like someone "descending into her own life."
But instead of "the pathos of kindled hopes,"
I feel this moment as something that imperils her,
something she's helpless to defend against,
as though the film foreshadowed an assassin's bomb.
This feeling brings with it a desperate urge
to "roll back the film," which succeeds only
in slowing it down to a pace that further accentuates
the dread, as though the footage slowed
to capture the instant the bomb goes off. Each step
seems drawn out endlessly and echoes so
in memory that I almost think I can feel—in her—
that earth-bound, raw, quicksilver weight
a life takes on at the moment it ceases to be a life.

25.

And so it continues, day after day, this endless succession of moments culled haphazard from the staticky dark. As though each were an event unto itself. As though each inscribed some legible mark on the frail wax cylinder that kept alive a voice from the ever-receding past.

My sister at thirty or thirty-one stripping off table varnish
while her daughters nap on a folded towel beside her.

In the archangel section of the plaster cast gallery, she holds
her breath until the security guard stops looking her way.

Standing beside the photomat, staring at a strip of pictures, her
look of puzzlement slowly gives way to a look of recognition.

In the middle of the night (I was eight or nine at the time) I wake
to find her patting my head—because she just had a bad dream.

Visiting hours over, she returns down the hall to her hospital room,
head down, shoulders stooped, her hands clasped behind her neck.

That same morning, when she started to cry, she somehow
managed to distract herself by biting her nails until they bled.

Overjoyed to be finally going home, and then, mid-sentence, falling silent
at the thought of it, as though her mouth had been covered by a hand.

A warm spring night. A streetlamp beyond an open window.
Beneath the sill, a girl's hushed voice exhorting itself in whispers.

One morning she leaves the house before dawn. She doesn't take
the car. By noon, she finds herself in the business district of the city:

A taxi is waiting, the driver is holding the door for her, and it seems
that now, after all these years, she's about to take the journey of her life.

III

ABANDONED RAILWAY STATION

The agent's office like an abbey chancel.
The smell of wood smoke from the baggage stalls.
Large empty walls, and a water stain,
ultramarine, like a fresco of Perseus,
head in hand, fleeing the golden falchion.

The silence of thousands of last goodbyes.
A dried ink pad. Stanchioned ceiling.
And a cognate, terra-cotta dust over
everything, with the on-tiptoe atmosphere
of a *boule de neige* before it's shaken.

WING DIKE AT LOW WATER

1.

The Corps of Engineers bulldozed it out
from the limestone bluffs at a point between
a towhead and the shallows, a conscript
calm which pays out water so gradually
its scudding surface seems an image of
the mower's motion, of pale, upended
grain stalks tumbling heavily from the scythe.

2.

And yet somewhere below the light bevel
of its watercourse, an undercurrent
quarries through acres of sand, gouging out
a barge road in mute, invisible, in-
cessant bursts, which is how we imagine
conscience works, rivering the mind until
the mind's capacities are shaped by it.

3.

To make of water a topiary:
declensions in the form of the maple
samara, the slope-backed channel swimmer
shouldering a wave, embodied psalm sound,
hemstitch, a cat's hackle that's been worried clean.
Or Odysseus's arrow punched up
to the feathers in Antinoös's throat.

4.

As though in the air above it spirits
lingered, the drunk at midnight reenacts
(for friends who've given up calling him back)
the myth of the water-walker: braced
mid-river, his arms outreach the multitudes,
all suddenly assumed into the echo-
lalia streaming through him from the dark.

BELFAST ARIOSO
8.17.94

She stands in the kitchen preparing a roast.
He stands beside her uncorking the wine.
It's early evening; a live opera is playing
on the BBC. She's wearing a pair of earrings

he'd bought at the co-op the day before,
a red-leaded rectangular glass the sun
through the skylight can't inflame,
however brightly he'd imagined it would.

He pours a small glass for each of them,
she raises hers, and though I can't tell
what they're saying, it appears that she is singing
to him, and he is answering back in song.

Back and forth they sing to each other,
each in turn determined to fill the silence
settling around them like a story whose end
their song foretells. But whose story is it, after all?

Theirs? Ours? History's own, as history claims?
(In the opera, it usually belongs to the one
who's killed, a violence we perceive
as beauty.) She sets the timer on the oven clock.

He clears his throat with a second glass.
And now they're dancing, arm in arm,
dancing across the bare, swept flagstones
of the kitchen floor. It seems so familiar

who'd think to ask if they'll still be here
when the singing ends. Or, if not, if they'll
be summoned when the world applauds
the art of catastrophe their singing forms.

A TULIP IN WINTER

Your out-of-season hospital tulip still
brightens above its parti-colored foil.

Lacquered in lamplight, its fleshy leafage
could, conceivably, survive this way

a hundred days. A hundred days (imagine
that) to paint out the wallpaper harlequins,

uncane the cane-back rocking chair,
reclaim your green connection to a place

where flowers such as these are grown
to leave the living less impossibly alone.

from

The Perishing

(2004)

of nothing less, or more, or outside us,
or within, of absolute forgetfulness,
of all things most a life bereft, a plinth
of air, a winter snow-fed sun that's sensed
only in the figure of a passing thought,
or the realization of what we thought
of nothing for, that zeroing in
of a self beguiled and, wanting n-
othing, finds it wants it all the more.

GREENCASTLE

Prison lights across Lough Foyle.
Sea stones drying in a tin pan on the windowsill.
On the fold-out cot, Ben asleep,
His radio headphones still turned on.

LLANDUDNO

Rigged with a sea-shawl of twilight and mist,
The refurbished eighteenth-century boardwalk
Emptied of its visitors, the souvenir stands shut down,
And like the slate boat housed in a local museum,
Its broad-planked floor strained against the anchor
Of its history. But no telling what thoughts the mind withheld,
Or the body remembered, to find ourselves wrong-footed
And alive to four or five skinheads stepping from a stairwell
In the parking lot, their forearms barred with swastikas,
And embedded in the leather of their combat boots,
A crosshatch metalwork of razor blades.

CAFÉ SOCIETY

Scarfed in a thin umbrellaed shade more rose
Than golden now the sun has slipped
The steepled sundial of St.-Séverin, the ousted
Small-time military ruler, exiled in Paris
Since 1984, now takes his morning coffee
At the street-side tables of Les Deux Magots,
A habit he wouldn't have imagined safe
Even two or three years before. But like
That cool, affluent stream of stylish people
Who surround him there, politics has
Its passing fashions, and often these outings
Leave him with the melancholy thought
That no one anymore wants him dead.

And so, in time, he finds he's less inclined
To leave the narrowing shade of his table,
A fact not lost on the salmon-vested staff
He commands by tips doled out deliberately
With an air of moneyed complacence.
And so, in time, he has managed by a simple
Nod of the head, or a finger raised
To encircle the thin-glazed rim of his cup,
To alert them to the privilege of
Such services as he might require.
But nothing in history is ever lost.
And something about that mute exchange
Stirs like a spoon a case recorded
In a U.N. document years before.

One evening, for the benefit of three mothers
Who'd been summoned to watch
Through the open window of a barber shop,
A badly beaten *milicias* youth was carried inside,
Stripped of his clothes, and bound spread-eagle
To a tabletop. They'd thought, at first,
He might be the local riverman's son,
The one who trapped chameleons he'd then sell
For coins in the village square. But finally
They couldn't say for sure, for the battered body
Laid out that way had seemed, somehow,
Unreal to them, the bound limbs merely symbolical,
The bruised torso illumined like an altarpiece
By the light of a handheld kerosene lamp
Around which insects thronged and fell
In a flurry of gilt enamelings. And in that raw,
Unworldly glow, the commanding officer
Conveyed by a simple nod of his head, or a finger
Raised to trace an imaginary ring in the air,
When the shocks should be administered
From a jumper cable attached at one end
To the dry cell battery in a transport truck,
At the other end to the grotesquely swelling
Spectacle of the rebel soldier's genitals.

Of course, all of that happened years ago.
Its time has passed. And now the idle days,
So many he's given up keeping track,
Stack up like saucers on a tabletop.
And it's from their spent endowment
That he pushes back, lights his first cigarette

Of the morning, and makes his way unhampered
Through the lustral wash of people
On the Boulevard St.-Germain. A liquid element
That has come to be, in its haute bourgeois
Anonymity, an otherness he enters as easily
As the past now passes out of memory.

CAROUSEL

He'd just switched off the overhead light and stretched out
For a nap before dinner, the quiet end of a travel day.
A plastic cup of orange peels, an empty half-bottle
Of some sweet wine he'd found in the hotel mini-bar,
And he remembers too a car horn sounding, then laughter
And voices spilling out into the parking lot below.
And then a fight broke out. Two men, he imagined,
Around whom others formed the cordon of a makeshift ring,
Their threats and goadings followed by the heavy thud
Of blows. He called the front desk and they said they'd go,
But for what still seems the longest time, it did not stop.
And then it did. And then there was a sound like
Hose-water splashing off asphalt, a car door closing,
And what he thought he recognized as the slurred, parenthetic
Phrasings of a boardwalk carousel winding down.

THE ART OF THE LANDSCAPE
for Mark Strand

In Sebastião Salgado's photographs
Of Rwandan refugees in Tanzania,
A viewer gets lost momentarily in the epic,
Bosch-like register of death and human suffering.
The far-flung encampments of washpots,
Lean-tos, scattered rags, the emaciated,
Fly-ridden children, the scabbed, hollow-eyed
Men and women gathering twigs or skewering
Rats for a cook fire, a people who appear
To have wandered here across the salt expanse
Of a drought-stricken, uninhabitable earth.
And their suffering is not made less of
Than their suffering is, nor their stares
Made more consolable than we've come to expect
From a grief beyond the reach of mercy,
For everything about them, we realize,
Will go on forever and always.

And yet, somehow, in the face of this same
Unspeakable harm, a photographic fact
Distills the air with a gilt precipitate
Apportioned it by a sunrise that has opened up
A thin empyrean of golden light, the strata
Of cloud illumined with some vaulted aspect
Of sublimity such as one might see
In a nineteenth-century landscape painted
By Kensett or Whitteredge or Heade,
Though the light of those paintings outshines

A world composed in shades of everything
Except what's human. And isn't that, after all,
What worries us most about this picture?
A beauty unchastened by experience?
The idea that, with deliberate care,
With weighed precision, the photographer
Has taken the measure of some pale
Effulgence that falls with what is hardly grace
On the whole anonymous tragedy held
In the hollow of an outstretched hand?
Or is it more that this is a landscape
From which human suffering is not dispelled?
That theirs is a misery before which
The beautiful, however haphazard,
However unwilled, might insusceptibly
Make itself known? That contrary
To some line we've drawn between what
We honor and what deplore, the two
Might actually subsist somewhere
Within the province of each other's worlds?

A rent in memory, and *Time* recalls
Another photograph by a photojournalist
Freelancing shots around Kosovo.
In a small, poppy-filled clearing in the woods
Two hundred meters above the mountain village
Of Velika Krusa, he has stumbled on a Serbian
Soldier who, except for certain small details,
Seems poised above the history he's making,
Afloat in the ether of a storybook world
Where even the familiar seems make-believe.

For within that world the soldier is tensed
And bent to play an English rosewood
Upright piano whose burnished surface
Is haloed in the tailings of a winter sun.
To the right of him, there is stacked up
What appears to be an abandoned cache
Of musical instruments; to the left,
A mounded tarpaulin against which rests
A Russian Dragunov sniper's rifle
With a nightscope and box magazine.
There couldn't be more than an hour or so
Of daylight left. And were our visions
Keen enough, we could just make out,
Halfway up the mountainside, the access to
A shallow cave, and within that cave,
Hunkered together against the cold, what remains
Of a family of Albanian musicians
Whose upright piano the soldier plays.

The family—a grandmother and her brother,
A mother with her two daughters and son—
Has sheltered in the cave for eighteen days
On a week's supply of water and bread
And dried sausages. And so it happens
That beyond all sense, rising up through
The chill gradations of the mountain air,
The family hears, or imagines it hears,
The faint but recognizable chords
Of a Mozart concerto in D Minor.
And so surely does the music filter up
Off the valley floor that they can tell

From the luff of a single out-of-tune
G-flat key that *their* piano is the one
Being played, and that the person who plays it
Does so with exceptional tenderness
And care. So much so that, all the while
The music plays, they find themselves
Inclining nearer the mouth of the cave,
Leaning out into the fleet *andante*
Of each carefully articulated measure.
And for what still seems a moment pitched
Well beyond the reach of space and time,
They take it all in, the thin, collecting overtones,
The loosely modulating lilts and falls,
The trills and tailed *arpeggios*, they take it all in
And hold it there, as if the weight of each note
Could quicken the minds' capacities,
As if the mind could actually abide such things
As a sniper's hands on the piano keys
Of a Mozart concerto in D Minor.

THE MONUMENT

From the legions they raised against him, Tamerlane built
His fabled wall of blood and bone, but in order to cast
   its shadow over
The warrior kings to come, he killed those left behind as well.

In 1915 the Young Turks counting heads conceived an epoch-
Making joke: How many Armenians does it take to build a wall
Ten times that which Tamerlane built from the body parts of men?

But the answer was monumental, the answer was something
Heretofore unimaginable on such grand scale, the answer,
They knew, was modern: Eventually they'd have to kill them all.

Decades later, having counted up the Jews, Hitler begins
   to brood,
"For who," he asks his cabinet "remembers the Armenians
   anymore?"
And even if they did not exist, even if they had never existed,

The Gypsies and homosexuals, the Freemasons, J.W.s,
   dabblers in art
When added to that already numberless sum might easily make
A shadow of Tamerlane's storied wall of blood and bone;

So next he figures the Christians in, and those who might be
   faint of heart,
The listless, the stutterers, the bookish and halt, and he
   figures how

(With the help of a roach poison, Zyklon B) he might actually
    kill them all.

And so the wall continued to rise, and so the wall, as if framed
And lighted in a photo by Leni Riefenstahl, overrode
    its lagging history,
Even though history did not exist, even though it has
    never existed.

In the Soviet Union the bourgeoisie is Lenin's self-
    appointed task,
So when Stalin takes over the job's been done with greater skill
Than Tamerlane dreamed could raise a wall from blood
    and bone;

Nevertheless, Stalin will go on tracking them down, in the parks
    and cafés,
Among sporting groups and writers' guilds, factory heads
    and Party leaders,
He will go on killing them, too, eventually he will kill them all,

Until the wall makes a relic of the Führer's dream, for it's a wall
Composed (just imagine it) from the corpus of one's
    own citizens,
Even though citizens did not exist, even though they had never
    existed.

So when Mao makes war on the landlords and intellectuals,
    the pacifists
And sly imperialist spies, when even where they do not exist
He mortars them into his own Great Wall of severed limbs,

He conceives of it as possible, so unnumbering are his kind,
To refigure a wall that's all on earth still visible from the moon,
If only he can go on killing them, if only he can kill them all.

And ever higher it grows, well beyond the reach of thought
    itself,
Until sheltered in the jungle one afternoon a man named Pol Pot
Speculates how, even if they do not exist, even if they have
    never existed,

He could eliminate all who ever wore glasses, or brewed sweet tea,
Or whistled a tune, the zeroes spiraling off his pen like the cries
Of the dead, the *O O O*'s that no one not even God can hear,
For as Tamerlane in his providence knew, the wall is the wall
Of oblivion, and even if it did not exist, even if it had never
    existed,
We'd have had to kill them anyway, we'd have had to kill
    them all.

STRANGER AT THE ASHWOOD THRESHOLD

1.

Did he think that disguise would fool me? Gathering about
His balding head those filthy rags? Poor-mouthing
His way beside my fire, then gazing into the looking glass
Of my bride's mind to summon up the legend
I'd seen last at the ashwood threshold twenty years before?
The husband who'd upped and sailed away on a black,
Oar-swept ship of war to a place he called . . . I call *Destroy*.

"Your son will vouch for me," he said. "I saw your king
On foreign soil. He wore a wine-dark, woolen cape
Fastened by a brooch inlaid with gold, a brooch on which
A great hound clenched and throttled to death a dappled fawn."
He knew, of course, I'd given Odysseus that very cape.
Had dyed its wool that royal red. Had buckled its folds
With that same brooch. And so, I suppose, I passed his test.

The salt tears soaked my cheeks. A fact he took in warily
Beneath his rags. Though how could I not have recognized him
With his poet's words, his poet's unfazed self-concern
So skillfully playing my emotions? The truth is,
However much I loved that man in the wine-dark cape,
However much I'd longed for him, I'd have settled
For the man with thinning hair, the beggar-king of Ithaca.

2.

Having slept alone for all those years in the upper story
Of our high-roofed home, having wakened nightly
In that rooted, rightly far-famed bed he built by hand
Around the bole of a thickset olive tree, I soon
Found out there are two known gates through which
All dreams must come to pass. The first is made
Of ivory, cleanly carved, the second of polished horn.

Through ivory our dreams are will-o'-the-wisps,
Scant tracings on the air; through horn they're star-signs
We'd be wise to chart our futures by. It was through horn
It came that night he questioned me beside the fire,
The contest of twelve axes, one for each month
Of the year I'd lived through twenty times for him,
House-bound to the labor of my hardwood loom.

The thwarted suitors watched in awe. He watched
Them watch, though none of them saw the hand
That strung his bow recalled my own hand spooling out
Raw wool, that drew on strength enough to strike
An arrow clean through all twelve blades recalled the heart
It took each night to mount the stairs, to climb back
Into the vaulted tomb of our empty, tree-housed bed.

3.

Waiting at the window while I braided my hair,
Odysseus stood and stared across the unraked grounds
He'd trashed at last night's welcome home.
One guttering pine-pitch torch still burned, its pool
Of light translated to a ringing lyre—the singer's who
Had begged for him to curb his taste for blood, to spare
One soul from among that haul of slaughtered men.

He'd been every inch the hero then, spattered
With gore, his forehead glistening, dripping red.
But this morning he looked like the man who stood
Beside me on our wedding day. His thin shirt clung
Like onion skin to his boxer's muscled chest and arms,
And as before, those faraway, slightly moonstruck eyes
Seemed focused on a flyspeck at the world's end.

It hit me then that, even as he stood there waiting,
Steeped in the memory of all this place brought home
To him, he labored at the anchor of whatever in me
Refused that death his life still longed to overthrow.
And I could see it coming, his going away, those
Maddened gulls scavenging after his trim black ship,
My harbored longings once more driven beyond his reach.

DRIFTWOOD

Tumbled from the backwash of a fishing boat,
Laved in salt and damascened with worm-
Loops scrolling the long arm's length of it,
It rehearses in our son's storied hands
A history of fells and sail-roads, of flare-ups,
Strongholds, the terror-monger at last laid low
And the gold hoard hauled from its barrow.
Stripped from the tree of reckoning, arrayed
Against the world's unpunished harms,
May it still serve in the coming years to bolster
The peacemaker's heart in him, to steer him
Around whatever new perils must now
Precede the homecoming folktales tell us is
The end-all meaning of our journeying.

HYMN TO NECESSITY

With a chain saw and axe, I spent a long
Morning cutting up a sycamore the storm
Brought down. For all twelve years we've lived here,
It has shaded over the kitchen window, upheld
Various clotheslines, feeders, rope-plank swings,
The candlelit rice paper Japanese lanterns,
And even one summer one corner
Of a straw-hooped canopy for a wedding.
So borne in mind, I've come to find that,
Rinsing dishes in the sink at lunch,
The space it opened over-brims itself
And turns what's not there outside in.
But how good the sun feels in its absence,
And how like absence to surprise me this way.

SMALL VARIATIONS

1.

In the Hospice gardens, midday in the bright sun,
A woman of thirty or thirty-five, too weak,
Exhausted, or disinclined to walk the few yards
Back to her room, raises her pale blue hospital gown
And in one slow motion squats along the pathway to pee.
And standing there beside her, her hopelessly
Embarrassed father, unable to look, unable not to look.

2.

The lamp turned off, the curtains white in folds,
First an ear, an eyebrow, the curve of her shoulder,
The small scallop of her collarbone, and slowly
His dead wife appears to him, just as she'd done
Thirty years before when he'd take the night train
Home from the Clinic, thinking his way through
The sequence of kisses he'd give her on his return.

3.

For days on end she sits beside her sleeping son,
Her fingers busily stitching and unstitching
A large needlepoint picture of an alpine cabin
Banked in snow. But how to explain the shame
That now comes over her? The shame that she'd
Already begun (even as he lies dying) to imagine
A world in which she couldn't imagine him.

4.

Twice that night he awakened to the soughing sound of rain
And twice discovered it was only that, across the street,
The recently widowed neighbor had left her garden
Sprinkler on, its standing water here and there welling up over
The concrete curb in loose, collected rivulets of wet,
A moonlit runoff less like spilled water than the dispossessing
Ghost of water sluicing down the gutter and away.

A MOMENT

What I perceived is what I remember.

I didn't know her name.
She was thirteen or fourteen, I was twelve,
And we were somewhere in California.

Her family had rented a campsite
On the lake side of a trailer park,
Their sky blue octagonal tent
Opening out on the water.

We'd spent all morning at the archery range,
And all morning our lead-
Tipped arrows traced
A liquid silence through the summer air,

Some errant, some true, some steered
As if by fortune toward
The banked-up bales of hay.

When she slipped away in the afternoon
I watched her growing smaller
as she hurried down the trail.

On the lake, an older couple in a red canoe
Rowed out toward the opposite shore,
And with each inaudible oar-stroke
The insect *chirrr* increased.

And then, from a cloudless sky,
A light rain fell.

I heard it fall, passing across
Wide water onto land, the warm droplets
Dimpling the trail with muffled,
Inexpressive thumps.

And without any thought of why or how,

I felt that moment take hold
In me, a moment
Without feeling or significance or form.

A WRITER'S LIFE
for Charles Wright

My dearest Anne,
                    How kind of you to take
The time to write and catch me up on things.
I miss so much our lunches after class, our talks,
Our walks along the river with your dogs.
And though I hold you dear in different ways,
You've become what I had hoped my daughter
Would become, were she alive today,
A companion with whom what narrow insights
Old-age affords might be exchanged
For that wide and mirrory outlook
Which now crowns your youth.
But she is not alive, nor is my darling James,
And so it is, from time to time, I think of you
As one of them. I hope you don't mind,
Or mind too much, for it's in that spirit
That I'll ask you, after I return, to tell me more
About your plans to take up writing
Now that you have finished school.

You are, you know, the brightest student
I have ever had, and I'd think you could do
Anything you want. Which makes me wonder
If you really want a life that's so—so what?—
So *self-inflicted* as this one. Looking back
On fifty-odd years of it, I feel the kind of
Resigned acceptance one might feel for
A small deformity, or a slight impediment

Of speech which, however politely it's received,
Nonetheless makes one think there's less
To lose by saying nothing. Be that as it may,
It's certainly true that writing provides
A "portal of escape" (the phrase, I believe,
Is Ruskin's) into some less tiresome
Version of ourselves.

                              Speaking of which,
You'll be amused to learn the Foundation
Has finally settled me into my very own
Ruined cottage, a stone, two-room
Fisherman's hut complete with a swaybacked
Roof that leaks, a rough wood floor,
And holes in the masonry large enough
To fire a sizeable cannonball through.
Creature comforts notwithstanding, I wake
Each morning perched atop a freshly windswept
Promontory three hundred feet above
The Irish Sea, a shelving aerie from which,
Whenever the weather breaks, I can see
All the way to the Isle of Man and across
To Galloway. On certain days it feels as if
I viewed the world from the highest reach
Of human consciousness, a view like that
Which Wordsworth claimed, looking down
On Chamouny from the Alps, made "rich amends"
(Though amends for what I can't recall).

Unfortunately, the weather hardly ever breaks,
For beyond all that there's not much here
But sheep and us. Which prompts me to say,

It didn't take long to fall back into the sheepish
Habits of our little flock. I write all day
Then pass the evenings in the guarded amity
Common, I suppose, to writers' retreats
All over the globe. The dinners are served up
"Family style"—roasted chickens, legs of lamb,
Heaping bowls of boiled spuds laid out
By six in the dining hall of a renovated
Fifteenth-century castle we've nicknamed
"Fortress Hunger." (The way we eat
You'd think we actually spent our days
Plodding behind a horse and plow.)
And afterwards, a turf fire banked
Against the chill, we're invited to gather
In the sitting room for some pinochle
And inchoate chat.
                          Lately, however, I find
I'm more inclined to watch, from a wingback
Chair beside the fire, the lighted city
Of an outgoing ferry crossing the horizon
Toward Scotland. It departs from Larne
Each night at nine, the final passage of the day,
I'm told, and it takes about three-quarters
Of an hour to slide across the windowpane
And disappear from sight. A great
Birthday cake of a ship with SEALINK
Blazoned along its side, it moves so slowly
It's hard to tell it moves at all. Still,
While it first sets off so brightly prinked
With running lights and cabin shine
It casts a green-gold shadow on the sea,

It soon burns down to a smoldering glow,
Snuffed-out like a candle flame. One curious
Thing about it is, no matter how hard I try,
No matter how fully I focus my attention,
I can never actually *see* it fade, never make out
Even one of those thousand fine gradations,
Even one of those incremental shifts
By which it finally disappears.
                              This will, I fear,
Sound strange to you, but it's as though
Throughout that brief excursion, that all-too-
Fleeting sleight of hand, I watched from afar
My own life pass across the windowpane,
How it set out glamored in the burnished hope
Of what they used to call "my gift," a sort of
Promissory note the Certitudes launched
Toward a future where, at journey's end,
It would be redeemed in a light like that
Which falls across the beeswaxed transoms
Of Vermeer. But the journey, it happens,
Is not toward such fulfillments. Nor have I ever
(As I recall) been touched by any such light.
It's more as if, little by little, in a slow
declension imperceptible to sense,
The mind's eclipsed, the promise dims,
And the light goes out altogether.
And then one day you find yourself
Alone and a little embarrassed
That you've dared outlive your gift.

But knowing your tendency to give
Such things your full consideration,
I suspect you've already made your list,
The pros and cons of the writer's life,
And held them in the balance. And lest
This letter settles too easily on one side,
I confess that if I had it to do over,
If I knew in advance what I know now,
I'd choose the same as I did then,
Though I hope you'll entertain the fact—
Or call it my strong impression—
That the supreme art is a happy life,
And a happy life anathema to art.

SUMMER SOLSTICE, ISLANDMAGEE

With water hauled up from a rocked wellhead,
You'd fieldwash your breasts and underarms
In the sink where the dinner dishes steamed
Then follow the late-setting sun to bed.

Bathed in lantern-light, our gabled room
Had one small window through which,
Refreshed, the sea wind amplified your nakedness
With the soft-bated breath of a Peeping Tom.

ROMEO & JULIET

With that same unsettling instinct for how
Human love can fall by chance to the borrowed
Grave of a coldwater flat, the forecast snows
Heaped up since dawn against our two small
Street-level windows, walling out the staticky,
Offstage noise of the early morning traffic,
The stink of trash and exhaust pipe fumes.
But when setting aside our breakfast trays
And throwing the bunched-up covers off,
You climbed up over me late for work and filled
My mouth with a nut-brown, poppied
Aureole, I couldn't believe that either of us
Would ever die, or that, given the choice,
We wouldn't choose this and be buried alive.

THE TALKING CURE

> *It exceeds all sorrows to tell you this,*
> *To recount in the face of such misery*
> *My little moment of remembered bliss.*
> —*Inferno*

Eyes shut. Lapsed time. The 2 a.m. aquarium glow.
The background noise of my parents' party
Winding up downstairs—nothing more
Than the usual things, laughter, commotion,
Voices lowered, voices raised, voices calling across
The room. And music, too, as I think back,
Though I heard it only as a thumping sound,
Like something in the walls, like a heart or something
Thumping in the walls. Was that, perhaps,
What awakened me? All I can say is I found myself
Suspended within that blue-green glow
The aquarium cast in the darkness of my room.

A ghosted room, as it turned out, for suddenly
A softly spoken voice appeared beside my bed.
Shhh, shhh, the voice said, *it's only me,*
Though I couldn't imagine who "me" might be.
Before I was able to ask, she passed a finger across
My lips and held it there. And when she took it away,
She pressed her mouth on mine. She lifted
My head. She kissed my eyes. She kissed my face
And neck. And then, in one slow continuous
Motion she unfastened a pearl-snap button
On her blouse and guided my hand inside.

How did I feel about that? Do you mean,
What did I *think* about how I felt? The truth is,
I have no idea what I thought, or even if I thought
At all, for it seemed so much a part of me,
What happened when she eased my hand
To a place I could only conceive of as a vacancy,
A chill alongside that rounded fullness
She had moved it from. She drew it, you see,
Along the raised abrasion of a surgical scar
That cut in a transverse angle from her rib cage
To her shoulder. And that she later told me
Was the reason she'd come, the reason
She'd left the party downstairs, the reason
She'd simply wanted me to look at her,
Wanted me to look and see the body
Her husband refused to see.

                    But could that
Really have happened? I wondered about it even then.
And how could it possibly end in tears?
The tears that all too readily came when she finally
Stepped back from my side, let fall her blouse
And underthings, and stood there lighted
By a sorrow pitched well beyond the reach
Of my thirteen years. And this is where I ask myself
If all of this was only a fantasy, just another
Freak, enciphered scene that rises to the surface
Of an adolescent dream. Believing that,
My parents both earnestly stood their ground
The following fall when her husband found her,

Four months pregnant, sprawled out naked
On the bathroom floor beside an empty bottle
Of Nembutal.

                  Of course, I talked to people about it
When things came to light. One caseworker
In particular took the better part of an afternoon
To explain why whatever this woman did,
Whatever had passed between us since,
Had nothing to do with love at all, not with
"Real" love anyway, but with something more—
How did he put it?—"unnatural," I think,
Though clearly he meant to say "perverse."
I accepted that. I saw the sense. But what I recall—
And, admittedly, it took me years to sort
What's fact from fiction—what I recall is that,
As she stood there figured in the watery glow
Her ever-receding memory casts,
I swam out to her to be taken up by the current
Of her inclining arms, to be folded back into
Another world where my own tears started,
Though what I wept for I can't say—*that* is what
I remember. That and the more unlikely fact
That all of this happened even as she was somehow
Muffling the sounds I could not keep down,
Easing me under and taking me in, lowering me
Into the mind's all suddenly silvered light,
And inside that to a welling in the blood,
A fullness in the heart, the secret, solitary
Nowhere of a place where in one brief fluorescing

Rush a shudder of grief and arousal struck
A lifelong, inwrought echoing chord.

I can tell by the way you peer up over
Your glasses that you're probably wondering why,
In thirty-five years of marriage, I never told my wife
About any of this. But let me ask you something,
Now that our session has come to an end,
Now that I've chattered on and on while you,
As usual, say nothing. Let me ask if you and the others
In your profession don't sometimes feel
Like the ones to whom it has devolved—from God,
No less—to serve as custodians for our souls?
The ones who keep from raveling into oblivion
That elaborate tapestry of self-delusions
Upon which our community now depends
For moral and spiritual guidance? No, I didn't think
You'd answer that. You're right not to, of course.

And so, the reason I never told my wife.
It's simple really. I just didn't want to hurt her.
I know you'll say my not telling her
Has hurt her more, but it seems to me,
Despite that conventional wisdom, some truths
Can do more harm than good. Or maybe
I've only come to feel, as time has passed,
That we understand less than we pretend
About how to love, or why we should, or what
We ought to expect from it. And who's to say,

Given the passionless affections, the pent-up
Malice and forbearance with which most couples
Tend to treat each other for the better part
Of their married lives, who's to say that what I had
With that poor woman years ago wasn't actually
Love of a finer kind than I've known since,
Or am ever likely to know again?

New Poems

I

SHADOWS OVER SHADOWS

In the sand, footprints stand around a burnt-out fire.

In the wind cave's prehistoric dark,
the stench of urine, the coldness of rusting chain.

Fog, then no fog, then sunlight, then fog.

Out in the bay, floating atolls
of giant kelp beneath which divers

search the ruins of a sunken city.

SOUTHERN GOTHIC

Poor white and pining, the full moon coins
its water-buckled image on a welling tide
that rakes the shingle back across the strand,
a bone-clatter by which fate decides
the youngest child in a family of nine
will be the first to die (the date marked
by an asterisk in the family Bible
that records such things) from illness,
or an overdose, or a traffic accident.

CATHEDRAL

1.

Time told. The city sacked. The conversation
come to an end. From the catslide, slate-
roofed belfry, the echo of the ghosted carillon.
Through the rose and lancet windows (where
not boarded over or crazed), the heaven-
haunted sun. Through the bronze, foliated
portal, the shadow of an architectonic god.

2.

A condom hangs from a nail in the apse.
On the mantel above the four-panel door to the vestry,
an engraved plaque a pocketknife scored:
"Memoriam: Fr. Anthony ~~Heath~~ ~~Riddick~~dick."
And all of it lorded over by the seraphim
on the paneled walls, one with massive, spray-
painted breasts, another with an inked-in vagina.

3.

The giant recumbent body sleeps and in
imagination seems to dream, and in that dream
there still resounds the after-words of devotion,
the low concentrated murmur of prayers,
the rustlings of communion, the hushed,
reverberant amens. All the soul-saving ministries
by which even we could forgive ourselves.

4.

From a distance one might easily think that,
anchored out of its element, an unmoored ship
had foundered there when the tidal surge
withdrew. How slow the unloading must've been,
and after, the shored-up cornerstone chained,
how heavy the labored tug-of-war as all dug in
and bent to haul the landlocked body overland.

THE OLIVE STUMP

1.

When hearing the name of Turnus,
Aeneas leapt the high walls of the citadel
and took the field, the crimsoned warring soldiers
might've marveled, might've set aside their shields
and dropped their battering rams, but they couldn't
have been surprised. The open ground was cleared.

2.

An old wild olive surviving shipwrecked
seamen had for centuries fixed with offerings to
a sheltering god was cut down with the rest and left
a stump. The gods overlook a lot of things, but not
a slight. Aeneas's launched spearhead buried itself
in that tough wood and the hero could not rearm.

3.

At least until a siding spirit intervened and broke
the bite. The hero weighed his heavy weapon
and towered up again. We're not told if
the olive bled, or if it wept. Like the man
who clung to the lead pipe a Hutu soldier used
to beat his wife and son, it was beside the point.

4.

Meanwhile, the upper hand was hammered out
by the powers that be. The scales were lifted,
balanced, trued. The fight's outcome was settled on.
Who knows what happened to the olive stump,
or to the family of the man the Hutu soldier
dragged outdoors, doused with kerosene and burned.

NIETZSCHE AT 44

He worried aloud that he'd buried a God
already loaded underground.
What worse than to think
belatedly?

Or perhaps,
as a disbeliever in angels,
he feared he'd have to invent them again.
But how?
And in what form?
And what bulwark against the unbearable?

Having abandoned art, history,
metaphysics, friends, having railed against
his family ("that infernal machine")
and ordained the ape the monarch of human nature,
there wasn't much left to do.

"It's really quite empty around me."

All in all, that's not a bad thing
for a philosopher, though it's not so good
for the man inside.
His head ached.
The Turin winter came and went.
He fashioned himself a man about town
then danced like a naked Greek in his room.

One afternoon in a merchant's house,
he opened a Gutenberg Bible
to find a sewing machine inside.
To Jacob Burckhardt he wrote,
"I'd rather be a Basel professor than God."
But then, of course, he'd resigned
his Basel professorship as well.

ORPHEUS & EURYDICE BACK HOME IN THE WORLD

Unable any longer to explain themselves,
they walked the neighborhood
in silence, each one lost
in the other one's thoughts.

A dog with a saffron bow on its head
passed them on the left.
A moment later, another dog,
this one in a leopard skin shawl,
passed them on the right.

A man who lugged an oversized
rolling garment bag
approached them to ask directions.

The street sweeper swept.
A cop unlocked the big iron bolt
on the transport van.

In the park, a wide expanse
of fresh-cut grass offset
the darker shades of green
beneath the oak and rowan and poplar trees,
the elm wound round with ivy,
the willow's trailing, downcast limbs
a Chinese poet once imagined
were the arms of a girl.

Perhaps they paused
to enjoy the sun.
Perhaps they continued on their way.

Did it matter?

Abandonment
was out of the question now.
As were grief, wonderment, tragedy.

THE GREAT GOD PAN IS DEAD

In winter coats the couples arrived
sharing a single umbrella. Others fended off
the sleety rain with hats, newspapers, and scarves.
In the foyer, they took off their overcoats
in silence, though the men were especially solicitous,
and the women left alone to ponder their thoughts
were careful to avoid each other's eyes.
As if stooping beneath a threshold, they bowed
before they entered the room where everyone
gathered into haphazard groups of threes and fours.
They stood that way for a very long time,
and since no one could think what else to do,
some of them wept, some of them prayed,
some of them simply stared outside
as ice flowers formed on the windows,
and the sleet turned slowly to snow.

SOUL

An oil-blacked
sea bird swabbed

with towels, dropper-
fed with a liquid

charcoal-glucose mix,
rightened, sized,

fattened on sprats,
then rinsed in a pail

of soapy water
and released back

into the wild.

II

ARE YOU NOW OR HAVE YOU EVER BEEN

When I emerged from the hospital annex,
the rain had stopped, and though numerous umbrellas
still floated past, the streets were starting to dry.
As the sun struggled to part the last remaining clouds,
a slight vibration in the courtyard caused
by an idling transport van traveled up through
the soles of my feet and joined a slight vibration
in my hands. Perhaps the life of sensation
had already returned, the life that in my time away
I'd often stood back and reflected on.

*

Without shading my eyes, it was difficult
to make out where I was, though each step I took
the closer to home I felt. Relieved in any case
to be alone (but relieved of what—responsibility?)
I no longer cared, it no longer mattered,
which way I turned, right or left, forward or back,
in the end I'd arrive at my apartment door.

*

A taxi pulled up in front of me and a woman
beside me stepped in. Across the street,
a man handing out leaflets did so standing
on the balls of his feet. What I'd thought
was the smell of dampened ash turned out

to be sweat from a window washer, his squeegee
canted like a guillotine, at the telecom office
next door. Even more significantly,
each of those images seemed to arrive
of its own accord (not "seemed," of course,
but "did"), and I was there, not to witness
but to "behold" it as it came. Was I,
I wondered, spilling over into the world,
or was the world spilling over into me?

*

Each session I entered with what I was told
were "natural" feelings of dread, each session
I left with mixed emotions of anger,
anxiety, pettiness, conceit, emotions
whose meanings "remained to be seen,"
or at least seen from a "broader perspective,"
for something somewhere inside of me
was always worth learning more about.
Nevertheless, there were days when I felt that,
easily enough, I might actually kill someone,
anyone, to escape whatever those meanings were.

*

My head heavy sometimes, sometimes light.
Sitting at my desk, teacup on the left,
stack of loose-leaf paper on the right,
I couldn't always tell if a minute or an hour
had passed between one line and the next.

In the afternoon, when asked how I was doing,
I answered, "I don't feel quite myself,"
though even as I said it I remembered how,
as a child, I'd happily exchange whoever
"I was" for whoever "I pretended to be":
daredevil, cowboy, private detective, etc.

*

Having breakfast in a local coffee shop,
the brief but nonetheless cheerful thought
that whatever came next would come for the sake
of appearances, and only as a way of distracting
my attention. In on the secret, the waitress
who brought the coffee spoke in the low, island
patois of characters in a South Seas tale.

*

At the sound of the approaching subway train,
the sitters stood up at the same time, the standers
stepped forward at the same time, at the same time
the newspaper readers folded their papers,
the parents took their children's hands.
Once the train came to a stop, all of us
like-minded people stepped into our individual lives
where an inspired theatricality prevailed:

*

A man with a tracheal breathing tube,
his sunburned face covered with stubble

as though he'd just returned from a climb.
A teenage girl, her eyes closed, her hands
folded in her lap, the new tattoo on her ankle—
a Zoroastrian Ram?—still raw and slightly
inflamed. A Marine with the laces of his desert-
issue boots untied (a coded protest against the war
slipped through the bars of my cell?). A woman
who moved her lips as she read but never
turned the page. A couple so happy, so at home
in their happiness, they might've been taken
right out of a Renoir boating-party scene.

*

The childlike reassurance I felt when,
as if turning back to a passage in a book
and reading it all over again, she answered
my questions the same way, with the same words,
the same turns of phrase and gesture,
that she'd answered them with the week before.

*

More squatter than bird, dozens of sparrows
perched along a cross-street telephone line,
their wing-barred feathers tucked against the wind.
One or two newly arrived, one or two lifted
and settled back, most of them never stirred.
When I stopped to think about it—that is,
when I waited at the curb for the light to change—
it didn't seem all that hard to imagine

that a saint once liked to preach to birds,
or that birds once gathered to listen.
Certainly, it wasn't any more implausible
than a hundred other things that crossed
my mind in the course of an average day.

*

In the morning, in the sun, in a public park
with a book, *Come Dance with Kitty Stobling.*
And a small boy beside me who asked if I'd like
to race him to the basketball courts and back.
When I told him I'm too old to race a boy like him,
his mother looked at me sharply, as though I'd knowingly
taken it upon myself to give her son a lesson in life.
"O tedious man with whom no gods commingle."

*

At an intersection where the farmer's market
had been set up in the morning, a line of cars
waited to turn at the crosswalk. There was
no light at the corner, and bustling about
with their plastic bags the pedestrians rarely
paused to let the traffic through. The driver
of the car at the head of the line was forced,
therefore, to nose forward into the crowd,
and as he did a loosely dividing channel formed,
a streamlet of people passed behind
and another passed in front of the car,
an encroachment played out in a series
of intricate feints and starts by which, at length,

the car crossed over to the other side.
In this way, a camel might pass
through a needle's eye, a thought that eased,
or at least momentarily compensated for,
the fear that I'd been watching all this
wholly independent of my will,
and with no more interest than I might've had
for any chance event that came my way.

*

At the station where I got on, an LED said
"Traffic normal through Cermak." And,
indeed, the lines at the turnstiles were normal,
the number of tourists in the concourse
was normal, normal too was the number
of occasional strangers who approached
with a look of such familiarity,
we passed with a friendly nod of the head.

*

I left my apartment in the afternoon, headed south
by a roundabout route to avoid the traffic,
crossed the river at State and continued downtown
to the public library. The Napoleon-red granite blocks
and high-arched windows, the Great Horned Owl
above the entrance, all were visible from a distance.
I was walking fast, working my way through the passersby,
and I seemed to arrive at each intersection
just as the light turned green. With everything
going so well, I continued on beyond

the library, slowed my pace and, as if
searching for an address, carefully studied
the numbers on the buildings along the way.

*

And then one morning a shadow fell,
in happiness or tranquility, the breath-held
physical sensation of it, fleeting, yes, an aftermath
already in the saying, but nonetheless there,
a spot of warmth that, because it depended
so little on me, spread throughout my body.
An emotion so tenuous it could only be experienced
by canceling out whatever emotions I already felt.

*

After a while, I thought myself away.
Or perhaps some random word or phrase
overrode my thoughts and an audible silence
filled my head. I could feel my heartbeat
through my shirt, the rise and fall
of my lungs, myself living on without me.
Myself not *for* but *as* the time being.

*

To take it for what it is, at face value.
To record it without making it into something.
To make it effortless, unconstrained, meaningless.
To escape the impression that what I see,
the images I respond to, are who I am,
and that everyone I notice is, at that moment,

who they appear to be. To keep to myself.
To do no harm. To know that tomorrow
I can try again. That was the dream,
that was the beginning, when I got
out of bed on a warm spring morning
in the middle of June. And for the next
few hours, that's what I attempted to do.

III

THE MEMORY-KEEPER

The smell of pine and bacon grease,
a house in a piney tract of land, a kitchen
in the house, a stove in the kitchen,
a skillet beneath which lowly burns
a bluish flame the jets discharge when a match
is held against their sound, a sound
that travels outside in from a metered box
where a boy sits watching the radium dials
record the backward passage of time,
and time itself, the beginning
of time, and beyond the beginning
the mind in the act of calling to mind.

8.9.08

The lake calm as a pond in the afternoon.
On a narrow street, the smell of humus
from newly potted lavender set out on pallets
at a flower stall. Later that evening, a corner booth
in a restaurant where the waiters, bartenders, busboys—
even, on occasion, the maître d'—kept picking up
glasses from the cleaning trays and shining them
with a towel. A grape arbor painted in the coffer
of the ceiling, and at the table next to mine,
a woman the arbor shaded from the sun.

PILSEN

In the empty soccer field bleachers, two day-
laborers listen to a radio in flame-resistant
chambray shirts. A PD tactical uniform
passes in a van. Beneath a leafless tree, a boy
in a Kashmiri shawl, and his far less political
girlfriend in unisex denim scrubs. Cyclists
in VizGuard vests. Skull-capped hawkers.
A beautiful Puerto Rican woman pushing
a stroller in camouflage pants. And foraging
trashcans looking for food, the same old man
with the Phuket helmet tied at the chin.
Not a single beret (unusual for this time of year),
but a cloche, a Fez, a Mardi Gras Horn Hat,
its yellow, green and indigo spikes tipped
with bells whose tinny chimes pass unheard
by the woman weeping (wearing her grief)
on a rusted wrought-iron bench.

A WOMAN NAMED THUCYDIDES

Having slept in a turnout in the backseat
of her car, she awoke before dawn, shivering,
hungover, unsure of where she was.
To her surprise, the sodium lights on the billboard
she had parked beside were no longer on.
Wind gusts, the smell of rain, the raw, unbroken
landscape like a field of ice. If this had been a movie,
someone would've been sitting up front,
someone who held her fate in his hands.
Though she couldn't see them, she could hear
birds passing overhead. Why do they even bother
to cross so vast and empty a space?
At the moment, none of the usual explanations
made sense. Her head ached, her feet were cold,
she couldn't find the words. And the man up front,
what did he think? What would he do?
Must something still happen before the end?

AN ORDINARY EVENING IN ST. PETERSBURG

May 5. Returned home.
—Chekhov's notebook

Walking back from an outdoor festival,
he cut through an alley
behind the Bureau of Public Works.

Halfway down the alley,
a metal barrel collected
a stream of oily water
that spilled from a pipe in the wall.

The water was warm
and steam rose off it, though
the barrel itself
was cold.

The noise of the street
seemed not to penetrate the alley,
so the splash of water
was just as audible
as the jets in the Fountain of Lions
he'd visited that afternoon,

a fountain where,
for lack of anything better to do,
he'd spent some time
trying to recall each of the thirteen
tramway stops
he'd passed along the way.

Because none of this
was out of the ordinary,
the entry he made in his notebook
was followed by the date
and time of day.

And how gratifying it was
to hold the world fast,
to record it without literature
to get in its way.
It was as if, between
what we perceive
and how we perceive it,
an adjective had been inserted,

and the word's work was to erase
that word.

BLINDNESS

On the opening pages of a novel she bought
at an English bookstore near the Seine (the famous, fading,
hand-stamped imprint: *Kilometer Zero, Shakespeare Books*),
the author enters a Belgrade bar and asks if the song
he'd heard outside was played on a record or a radio.
At the time, the owner of the book was seated in the cabin
of a passenger train as it labored through the mountain forests
on the Franco-Iberian frontier. Having deciphered
and then politely refused the mute gestures she'd directed
toward the vacant seat beside her, a family of four
had crowded together on the opposite, backward-facing bench.
The daughters were settled at either end and all four
stared in silence as the landscape blurred and disappeared
in the tunneling dark beyond. The daughters' boots
were newly polished though the mother's were scraped
along one side as though she suffered an affliction of the legs.
At various stages in the journey, the father produced
a silver, hand-wound pocket watch and, tapping on its glass,
pointed out the time to the daughters. Whenever the train
crossed a bridge, it slowed enough that the river below
reflected the sun so brightly that it took a moment
for their eyes to adjust, a moment of blindness
     they happily shared—
even though they shared it in silence—with the reader
sitting opposite them. On one such crossing, the river past,
the daughters watched the reader take a pencil out
and, much to their surprise (for their father would never

have permitted it), write down in the flyleaf of the book
I found at a library sale in Portland, Maine:

bridgewater

blindness

a family of four

Franco-Iberian fontier

VARIATION ON A THEME

1. The Pier

What she said was not what she meant to say.

As they side-stepped past
the rotting patches of giant kelp
the tide dragged up on the strand,

she held his hand, she admired
the fine-boned features of his face,
she studied the overlapping
shadows they cast.

He seemed less distant than preoccupied
(or was he simply shy?),
and his narrowing slightly cross-eyed stare
would rarely hold
on hers.

Nevertheless, two years younger,
she followed him into the shadows of the pier.
The joint, the condom,
the *in* not *out of* the body thing,
she'd heard about them
from the other girls,

though once they went their separate ways,
she was surprised to find
the throb of whatever she felt inside
was no bigger than a bottle fly.

2. Film Noir

A mist had settled over everything.

It was after ten, almost eleven.
A smudgy lamplight overran the curbs
where leaves had started
to gather as well.

Some young people
prowling the neighborhood
were afraid that nothing would happen tonight,
just as nothing
had happened the night before.

Although it was cold,
the boys wore cutoff sweatshirts,
and the girls,
more comfortably dressed for the weather,
kept laughing at the things the boys said.

A car turned onto Millbrook Road,
dimmed and then extinguished its lights
before rolling to a stop in the leaves.

When the young people passed,
they banged on the hood with their fists—
the boys, not the girls,

though the girls were amused by this as well—
and frightened the man inside.

Or did they?

The car door opened.
The man stepped out and,
as killers do in Hollywood films,
slipped a hand inside his coat.

And then, in a quiet, almost whisper
of a voice, he said something
none of them could hear,
though *how* he said it
was the thing he said.

Without looking back,
the young people kept on walking,
though faster now,
kicking up leaves as they went.

And when they were finally
far enough away they were sure
the man couldn't hear,
one boy turned and shouted back
"Oh yeah motherfucker,
we're really scared."

And that was that.
One of the girls drew closer to the boy
who'd said those words,
another drew farther away.

LIFE STUDY WITH TWO ENDINGS

1.

After driving all night through sleet and snow,
a formica tabletop warmed by sun in a coffee shop
near Keene. Inch by inch, an ice panel slides
from the corrugated roof of a pumping station across the road.
It's he who points it out to her, in a patch of thaw,
a northern cardinal beaking cinders looking for seed.
And now she remembers another cardinal perched on a branch
in an oil painting at the Cooper-Hewitt years before:
female, mated, a slash of coral along its tail, and the call
she happens to know it makes, the down-slurred whistle
that ends in a sliding three-note trill. Behind the counter,
the waitress has been watching: the wilderness between them,
the woman's unloosed, unwashed hair brushed back
and burning in the morning's newly warming sun.

2.

After the dishes were cleared from the long,
candlelit table set out on the lawn, she poured the coffee
and began to tell her story again. The seaside café.
A warm channel wind through an open door. The wines
of Samos and something about a sidelong glance
from the waiter that reminded her of a Byzantine panel
they'd seen that day. All in all, she believed that
they were happy then. Even when the café emptied out
they continued to follow the course of their journey
from here to there. And they were almost there, as close

to being there as they'd ever been, when someone
behind them whispered the lights out in the hurricanes
and the two-fold ending of their marriage began:
the pain that passed between them in the dark, the pain
that with each telling grows more abstract and historical.

A THEORY OF ABSOLUTE FORMS

He sketched with a pencil a luna moth he'd seen
drying its wings on a wooden panel of the potting shed.
The silence deepened and the pencil moved
of its own accord, beginning with the intersected span
and ending with a simple S-shaped bend where hindwing
turns to margin. When the pencil stopped, the luna
moth stirred but would not lift from the corkboard tile
where he'd mounted it with a dressmaker's pin.